# Memoir of a MISFIT CHEF

# Memoir of a
# MISFIT
# CHEF

## A Rise from the Ashes

First edition
PAUL ALVERO

# Acknowledgements

The world didn't just try to break me; I challenged it to, and it came close.

The most difficult part of writing this memoir was having to re-live it. Life wasn't always easy, but it's not supposed to be. You're supposed to be challenged.

I want to express my gratitude to my editor, Aimee Heckel. When I call her one of my best friends, I truly mean it. She was the first person I ever shared my whole story with, making her the first person to know everything about me. While editing this memoir, I texted her almost every day during a very challenging moment in my life. I already felt I had lost everything, and all I had left was a story.

Coming up in Vail was a lot of fun. Actually, we had a blast. I wish I could say, "and nobody died," but I can't. A lot of people did. I won't name them all, but these are the closest of close friends I have lost: Josh, Jesse, TJ, Johnny Tsuname, Joe, and my little brothers, Britton and Hoyle. You're my boy, Brit! And God Damn-it Fucking Whitmire, GDFW you sure knew how to live up to your nickname! Lost but not forgotten, I'm sure you're all up there shredding heaven's halfpipe. Rest in peace!

# Table of Contents

# Preface

I had just relocated to Las Vegas, enjoying a Miller High Life on the world-renowned Las Vegas Strip. I was at the AmeriCan Beer and Cocktails, located in the Linq Promenade and specializing in eco-friendly canned craft beers from around the world. I just wanted a High Life.

The Linq Promenade, a relatively new addition to the strip, was bustling with tourists and loud music. My phone rang. It was a man with a heavy French accent, and I could barely understand him. I asked him to text me his number; I'd have to call him back. I found a quieter space and did. The man on the line was Chef Jimmy, the executive chef of L'atelier de Joël Robuchon at the MGM Grand. The late Joël Robuchon, the highly acclaimed recipient of thirty-two Michelin stars—the most of any chef in the world. It was an honor to just get the call.

Chef Jimmy had a job opening and was inviting me in for a stage. I explained my experience doing tasting menus.

His response: "We don't do tastings. Our food is too precise."

I knew the restaurant specialized in tasting menus. However, I had applied for a master cook position. I didn't consider myself just a cook; I was a chef. But if a restaurant like this was not hiring, you couldn't apply. When I saw an opening, I went for it. I figured I just needed in the door.

The week after my stage, I was invited back to do a tasting. They said I was overqualified for the cook position. I had the validation I was looking for. I was a world-class chef. I had worked my way up to the top of the restaurant world.

MGM Resorts had just laid off nine hundred mid-level managers. I was offered just that: a chef position in a management role. I accepted the job, meaning I was now a chef for the highly acclaimed Joël Robuchon. Looking back on my life, it seemed impossible to imagine. I had been an outcast from day one. A degenerate punk. Society had never accepted me. So how did I get here?

I thought I'd never work corporate. I thought I'd never work in an open kitchen. Yet here I was working for a cooperation with 90,000 employees worldwide in a fully open kitchen of a Michelin-starred restaurant on the Las Vegas Strip. I guess you can't always predict the direction of your own story.

Four months after I started, MGM decided to close the restaurant for a couple of weeks mid-summer. The heat of the desert slows business and our kitchen needed some repairs. I took the opportunity for a vacation. I wanted a quiet, relaxing trip. I chose Sayulita Nayarit, Mexico. I had never been there, and it was exactly what I was looking for. Far from the glitz and the glam, I wanted to enjoy the simple life.

When I returned from vacation, one night I found myself sipping on an expensive glass of champagne while enjoying the views of the glittering Las Vegas Strip. I was in legendary chef Pierre Gagnaire's private dining room on the twenty-third floor of the Waldorf Astoria. High above the bustling strip it was peaceful, I felt like I had made it.

It was a mere five years after I had left the comforts and stability of a casual Italian kitchen to explore the world of fine dining. On this night, we had just finished service for an amazing collaboration dinner featuring the iconic dishes of Gagnaire and Robuchon. Three years earlier, I'd had dinner at Gagnaire's restaurant, looking for inspiration. Now, I had just cooked in his kitchen.

Our goal of the dinner was to honor two of the greatest chefs in the world by showcasing their contrasting styles in recreating the dishes of their past. For me, the standout dish was Gagnaire's steak tartare with mimosa salad and caviar. Unlike my previous experience as a guest, these were the dishes I expected to encounter at a Pierre Gagnaire restaurant.

As the two teams gathered in Gagnaire's private dining room, the GM struck up a conversation about smuggling drugs onto an airplane. This was a serious conversation, as Gagnaire was closing for two weeks and the general manager was taking a vacation. With the many degenerates I had associated with over the past forty years, I felt more than qualified to participate in the conversation. As I was close to chiming in with the suggestion of the swallowing of a drug-filled condom, I refrained. This was a conversation I didn't feel the need to be a part of.

The conversation then shifted to perving out on the freaky sex we could see in the adjacent building. Again, I was not amused. I had done more than my fair share of cocaine with strippers and sex in hot tubs. I didn't feel the need to share my crazy past. This job was a new start for me.

It is often considered a meaningful accomplishment to be the youngest to achieve culinary greatness, but the reality is that you need to be young. A youthful energy is a requirement. At age forty-one, I was past that.

Later, as I walked along Las Vegas Boulevard, I passed the Bellagio. DJ Tiësto blared over the stereo, and the fountains were dancing to *Footprints (All Over The World)*. I stood there watching the show, and I reminisced about my journey, from the unbelievable highs—wild yacht parties, five-star dining in foreign countries, cross-country skateboarding tours, the girls—to the lower-than-lows. Homelessness. Evictions and hunger. Chronic insomnia that could have destroyed it all. But it didn't. Against all odds, against anyone's expectations, I had not only survived, but I had thrived.

The most famous of all *Scarface* quotes crossed my mind: "The world is yours!" I felt the world was, indeed, mine.

# PART I

# Chapter 1:

## Burning Down the House

The day I set my house on fire changed everything. It burned nearly to the ground.

Although I was not the one who directly lit the match, I felt responsible. Maybe I was wrong to take the blame. After all, at eleven years old, I was the youngest in my group of friends. Yet I knew better. My friend Matt, who was a couple years older than me, would forever be known as "Matches." As for me, I would forever be known as a skater punk. People didn't expect much from a skater punk.

Skaters were viewed differently in the eighties. We were primarily thought of as vandals. One of our neighbors, in particular, had the smoothest driveway but would never let us skateboard on it. We didn't like that. Needless to say, we toilet papered her house on multiple occasions. That didn't make her like me more.

On this particular day, it was a couple years after the skateboarding movie *Thrashin'* came out. I had a vivid picture of the Daggers pouring gasoline on the Valley kids' vert ramp and lighting the thing on fire. I may have been young, but I was still a pretty smart kid and knew how flammable gasoline was. Regardless, I was still a young, punk skateboarder, and it looked like fun.

We decided to pour a little gasoline on the ground and light it on fire so we could ollie over it. Certain our neighbors would call the cops on us and get us in trouble, we had a brilliantly stupid idea. We decided to light this little fire in our garage, which was connected to the house. The first time, we were smarter and put a little gas in a cup first.

The next time—well, I was skateboarding outside on the driveway at the time, so I didn't fully see how it happened, but by the time I looked over, Matt was swinging around a three-foot ball of fire. Matt had decided to pour gasoline directly out of the can and onto the still-flaming puddle. I can't imagine what he expected would happen. Needless to say, Matt tossed the can and ran. The rest was history.

Until this day, our neighborhood was the envy of all others in town. I was viewed as a normal little kid, albeit with the "unfavorable" hobby of skateboarding. I lived a storybook childhood. In a neighborhood where all the little boys played innocent games with the little girls, this was the type of childhood people dreamed of—before adolescence, when hormones kicked in and playing with the opposite sex became taboo. Before the fire, if anything, among the other kids, I was considered innocent. I remember my friend Betsy's birthday party. She said something about her "birthday suit." At age five, I didn't know what she was talking about.

I replied, "I don't have a birthday suit."

Of course, she laughed at me for not knowing "birthday suit" meant "naked." I wasn't hurt by her laughter. I was confused. My parents were Filipino immigrants, still relatively new to this country. I found comfort in blaming them for not teaching me American culture.

One of my earliest memories of my dad was sitting on the back porch, watching him in awe. He nailed metal roller skate wheels to a two-by-four. A homemade scooter. Back then, I thought of my dad as an artist. He was creative. A handful of his oil paintings, mostly of nature scenes, hung around our house. Gorgeous pictures of lakes, streams, and trees. He was like Bob Ross with an extremely steady hand.

That wasn't how he made a living though. He was a doctor by trade, a heart specialist by profession—but that didn't last long. Rather early in his career things changed, probably for the better. I was young when my dad was taken to court for malpractice. I couldn't tell you the details of what happened, but the trial went all the way to the Supreme Court, eventually being ruled a draw and creating a lot of stress and costing our family a lot of money.

This would be my first experience of many with the American judicial system.

Back then, my dad was the only doctor in town. We had been drawn to the small farm town of Jackson in southern Minnesota, because we heard from a friend that the town needed a doctor. My dad had graduated from medical school in New York with a degree in cardiology, but now we were living among the corn fields and pastures of America's heartland.

Despite his degree, my dad was best known as a family doctor, not a specialist. He was also known as one of the most caring people in the world. That's what made him a great doctor. He would often wake up in the middle of the night to make house calls to the elderly of our town. Once, he accepted a dozen eggs from a farmer to cover what would have been a $75 dollar medical bill. That was a pretty expensive dozen eggs. My parents raised me to be humble and have great values—to deeply care for others.

My parents were religious; after all, they named me Paul and my middle name is Christian. But I wasn't the saint they were hoping for. They tried to ground me once, because I refused to go to church. Then they came home from church, and I was playing basketball at my neighbor's house. I was a devil child. They never tried to force me to go to church after that.

I will never forget the day I learned how to ollie in 1987. This was before the internet, and libraries were still full of books rather than tables full of computers. There were only a handful of skateboarders in my town, and none of us knew how to ollie. All the kids in my neighborhood were close friends, but my buddy Sean was my best. He got me into skateboarding. Just a few years earlier, Sean came knocking on my door, asking me to go bomb some hills with him. My parents had previously given me and my sister, Trina, Variflex skateboards along with Cabbage Patch Kids as presents. It didn't take long for me to trade Duncan the Cabbage Patch Kid to my sister for her skateboard.

By age nine, I was pretty confident with my hill-bombing skills. We made up our own downhill race, emulating the La Massacre—the last big downhill race—from the *Thrashin'* movie. I remember crashing through a stack of wood pallets. It made me feel tough. Bombing hills was one of the greatest feelings. I think I was simply a speed freak. However, on this summer day, Sean and I wanted to progress. We decided to go to the public library in our town (quite possibly our first time ever in a library). There, we found a book about skateboarding. In this book, of maybe twenty pages, we found a tutorial on how to ollie. With a slow-motion sequence shot, we learned the technique.

We learned the ollie was invented by a guy named Alan Gelfand, and it means "no hands." Alan invented the trick while skating in empty swimming pools and later Rodney Mullen took the trick to flat ground. Learning how to use momentum and foot coordination, Sean and I were now able to "jump" over or onto obstacles while our skateboards were magically stuck to our feet.

This basic trick, along with the creative minds of skateboarders, changed this childhood hobby of ours forever. We no longer viewed a curb, ledge, rail, or rock as obstacles. They were now features. During recess at school, we became the entertainment, as other kids would line up to watch us skate. Our bag of tricks was still pretty small; after all this was the eighties. Ollieing over little kids as they lay down was our greatest feat. That was how my elementary school recess was spent. I even began bringing some of my smaller launch ramps to school and hiding them in the bushes. I wasn't really hiding anything though. Everyone knew. Even the school aides were lining up to watch us skate.

Before learning how to use power tools, I remember "hippie jumping" around our driveway, usually with my favorite band, BonJovi, blaring in the background. We also made simple bank ramps by leaning pieces of plywood on boxes or blocks, whatever we could get our hands on. Skating off them or even just learning kick turns on them—these were my humble beginnings. Simple times.

Sean and I skateboarded around the neighborhood every day, whether it was bombing down hills or learning how to axle stall on curbs. It didn't matter; we just liked to skate. Even with all the natural obstacles around us, my greatest pleasure was building our own. I liked to work with my hands. I was becoming resourceful, too. I learned how to draw perfectly smooth transitions using a piece of string with a pencil tied on the end.

Our biggest challenge, however, was how to bend wood. Our first plan was actually the most imaginative (although least effective). We decided we would simply soak the sheets of plywood in water overnight or even several days. The soaking would soften up the wood just enough to allow the sheets to bend for our desired transitions. Thinner sheets of plywood were preferred, but we didn't really have that option. Although I'm not proud to admit it, most of the wood we used we stole from the nearby vocational school. We were just determined, little kids and wanted skate ramps. How much trouble could ten-year-olds get into anyway? Later we learned to use a circular saw and adjust the blade depth to about half the thickness of the wood and cut shallow slits along the grain two inches or so apart. We were young kids learning on our own.

This was all before the fire, when I was still considered the innocent son of immigrants. After the fire, none of the parents in the neighborhood would let their kids hang out with me.

I missed my childhood innocence. I remembered playing "cops and robbers," when we would actually fight over who got to be the cop. I always wanted to portray the "good guy." During the summers, we played what we called "night games." As far as I knew, we made most of these games up. Kick the Can was one of our favorites.

But now, our house had just burned to the ground, and I was being blamed. Overnight, it was as though I had been infected with cooties. I'm sure I wasn't the only kid involved with the fire who experienced this. I'm sure Matches felt like he had cooties, too. Now our whole neighborhood on the west end of town had an ominous feeling to it.

My brother, G.P., who is ten years older than me, had left for college by this point. At age seventeen, a year earlier than most. Lucky for me, I had inherited his classic, old-school silver boom box, the type you'd see the hip-hop thugs from the eighties carry on their shoulders walking down the city blocks of New York. With his boom box, I also inherited his cassette collection. The music he left me was the genre that affected my life greater than possibly anything. Hair bands, glam rock, BonJovi, Def Leppard, Whitesnake, Alice Cooper, Warrant, you name it. Not only did I love the music, but I also loved the lifestyle it represented. Partying like a rock star became my fascination. The sight of Tawny Kitaen in a white dress doing the splits across the hood of a car etched in my mind. I wanted to be a rock star. I wanted my own Tawny Kitaen.

After the smoke cleared, literally and figuratively, our house was rebuilt. I felt like I had aged ten years overnight. Although I was only eleven, I felt like I was twenty-one. There were no more "night games." The only thing that returned to my life was skateboarding. I had transitioned away from skateboarding launch ramps and homemade rail slides; those were a thing of my past.

As my friendship with Sean grew, we became the neighborhood troublemakers. We often went to our friend Monica's house and raided her parents' liquor cabinet. They must have worked a lot, because they were never home. We were still too young to actually drink, or at least I was. I remember going down by the creek and taking a swig of whiskey and spitting it out instantly. It left me wondering how people could actually drink the stuff. Sean was a few years older than I was, so it would be easy to blame him for many of my early "adult" experiences. That sip of whiskey was my first taste of alcohol—and I didn't like it.

At twelve years old, I was growing up quickly. Years earlier than typical teenagers, my house became the neighborhood hangout. I was "trouble," and my "bad boy" reputation was growing. And stealing booze wasn't the only havoc we were raising. Monica's house was the perfect hangout place, with a pool and hot tub. It was always somewhat of a free-for-all; Monica simply couldn't control us. One summer afternoon, some of the guys were in her room, presumably trying to "get to third base" with her. While the groping was going on, a couple of the other guys and I decided to try to recreate a scene from the movie *Thrashin'*, where they skateboarded on top of the roof. Monica's roof just happened to be easily accessible, so we climbed up and started skating around.

Meanwhile, while we skated circles around her roof, some of the non-skateboarders decided to raid the fridge and start a food fight. Sometime during this chaos, I got hit in the face with a frozen hotdog. The frozen wiener gave me a gushing nosebleed. Who would have thought the greatest danger while skateboarding on a rooftop would be frozen hotdogs? With my nose now pouring blood, I crawled off her roof and headed to the nearest restroom, leaving a long trail of blood down the side of her house and across her back deck. Needless to say, her parents were not pleased with us. This, of course, led to a scolding from my parents, as well. The result: We were never allowed to hang out at Monica's again.

Now in the early nineties, my house was the Skate Mecca of Jackson, with the nearly unskateable eight-foot vert ramp in the front yard and the ridiculously fun three-foot mini ramp in the backyard. Not to mention the random launch ramps all over the place. My parents didn't seem to care, not that they could have stopped me, anyway. But, during my skateboard punk days, our neighborhood was still growing. An empty lot had been cleared out for a new playground and right next to that lot, they were building a new house. That house was to become the new home for our insurance agent.

With the eight-foot vert ramp impossible to ignore and too much of a liability, he made us tear it down. The large ramp then curbed his curiosity, and he quickly learned of our three-foot ramp in the back. He told us to get rid of it, too, but the mini ramp was too much fun for any of us to destroy. Luckily, there was another skateboarder in town who we simply referred to as "W," a Vietnamese immigrant whose name was too difficult to pronounce. W lived halfway across town, far out of the sight from our insurance agent. So W's house became the new home for our beloved mini ramp.

Still, my house was the original skate house. I even had a micro ramp in my closet just like in *Gleaming the Cube*. Although I may never forgive him for destroying my childhood skate dreams, our new neighbors weren't all that bad. With our insurance agent also came two new kids to the neighborhood. One of those kids was a cute girl named Lexy. Lexy was sweet, and I would even go as far as to consider her my first real crush. One day, I stopped by her house and her dad had told me she was sick, but I tried to see her anyway. That's when I realized I genuinely cared about how she was doing. When you're only twelve, I don't know if you can really call it dating, but that was as close as we could get. At such a young age, it's crazy to think I already wanted a girl to keep me out of trouble.

# Chapter 2:

## Misfit on Snow

Somehow, I survived elementary school. By sixth grade, my group of friends was changing. Sean's dad had decided to move the family to Michigan because of a job opportunity, so I lost my best friend. Furthermore, most of my skateboarder friends were moving onto high school, as they were a few years older, and they were becoming disinterested in skateboarding.

My life, however, stayed its course. Middle school didn't seem much different than elementary school, and afternoon recesses still consisted of me skateboarding on one of my hidden launch ramps, now located in a park across the street from the middle school. To make things even better, W lived near the school on the same block, so I was able to skate my old ramp every day. I rarely found myself in my own neighborhood anymore.

I didn't like to be viewed as a hell-raiser, at least that was never my mission. I was just a skateboarder, a young one at that. One day, I stopped by to pick up a friend on my way to school. It was about a mile-long downhill ride from his house. I was zigzagging down the steep section to control my speed, and I happened to be on the wrong side of the road when a cop spotted me. He stopped me and confiscated my skateboard. The police held my skateboard in a jail cell for a week.

Yep. The cops locked my board behind bars.

When the week was over, with a parent present, I was allowed to bail my skateboard out. I was twelve years old, feeling harassed. How could a grown adult take away what was essentially a toy from a little boy? I felt bullied, and it left me with a negative opinion of authority figures.

A new gas station was being built in the center of town. The gas station had small banks made with fresh concrete and nice, recently painted curbs. One night, I was skateboarding at this gas station, doing little slappys on the painted curbs and a cop rolled up. My skater instincts from my previous experience with the cops was to just run; I wasn't letting them confiscate my skateboard again. So, I took off to a friend's house and knocked on the door.

"I need a place to hide," I blurted out.

My friend slammed the door in my face. I took off running again, finding shelter in some bushes. While hiding, I could hear the cop nearby. Suddenly, he shined a flashlight directly at me. I found myself trembling in fear, and all I could think was "Just don't look up. If I don't see him, he doesn't see me." I was terrified, but I felt an incredible adrenaline rush.

The cop eventually left. I felt like I had escaped from the police. At the time, it seemed like quite the feat. I felt proud. Thinking back, the cop must have seen me. How could he not have? Regardless, that was no way to treat a child. I should never have been chased in the first place.

After that, I never regained my trust in the police.

While I was graduating from elementary to middle school, my brother had graduated from the University of Minnesota with a business degree and landed a well-paying job as a financial adviser for what was then known as IDS, later Ameriprise. While working, he decided to continue his education and pursue his master's degree.

When I was younger, G.P. was rarely around. Our ten-year age difference was too big, although I do remember him picking on me a lot. One day, he threw me in the dryer. He would also lock me outside in the middle of winter while I was wearing nothing but underwear. Regardless, I always looked up to my brother when I was young, and he was a huge influence on me—maybe my greatest influence. When I was still rolling around on an entry-level Variflex skateboard, G.P. offered to buy me a new skateboard if I did five book reports. I gladly obliged.

When we did hang out, he often took me kneeboarding. He liked to listen to The Cars on our way to the lake, greatest hits like *Let the Good Times Roll* and *Magic*. Once, he took me to Spirit Lake. I'd heard rumors of people-eating piranhas in the lake. I tried not to show it, but I was terrified.

By the time I was ten, my brother became more like a father figure to me. My actual father was around, but he worked a lot, and so did my mom. Plus, I was the youngest child, so I think my parents were already exhausted with parenting by the time I came around. Then I burned down our house, and, well, I'm pretty sure they wanted to disown me.

Spending summers at the lake house largely defined my childhood. After the house fire, we had no choice but to stay at the lake house. So I built a nice four-foot quarter pipe on our driveway. Later, I built another four-foot mini ramp in the backyard. We also had a decent boat with a fifty horsepower outboard motor. Not much, but it worked for us. My dad also found a new obsession: personal watercraft. So he sold our snowmobiles and got several Jet Skis. First, he bought a Kawasaki X2, a cross between a sit-down and stand-up. Eventually, he bought two Kawasaki 550sx stand-up machines. That was my thing.

Stand-up Jet Ski racing became a dream of mine. We set up our own race courses with empty milk jugs, even using my sister's trainer kayak as a "log jump" obstacle. I was only thirteen years old, the legal age in Minnesota to operate watercraft by yourself. I just needed to pass a written exam. I easily did. My friends passed the exam, as well, so everyone was legal. As long as we all had our watercraft permits, my parents didn't care. Someone would just drop us off at the cabin and leave us for days or even weeks all summer long. At a young age, we were already given unsupervised freedom.

After the summer was over, harsh Minnesota winter kicked in. My brother continued on as my primary influence, taking me snow skiing for the first time. He took me to Mount Kato, about an hour and a half drive away from Jackson. Mount Kato, with its four hundred vertical feet and ten ski lifts, was a major upgrade from the hill my brother had learned on. The nearest ski slope to Jackson was in Estherville, Iowa. Essentially it was a small hill in an elderly couple's backyard. The backyard had one rope tow and was rarely open.

I actually didn't believe the resort was real. Until a few years later, when I finally got my driver's license. I decided to check it out with my friend, Josh. As we pulled up to the door in the early evening, it was pitch black. The hill definitely didn't look open, but we decided to knock on the door. To our surprise, someone answered. They gave us permission to check it out. Sure enough, there was what looked like a homemade rope tow along maybe a one-hundred-foot-long slope. I couldn't believe my eyes.

"This place is skiable?" I thought to myself.

By Christmas of 1989, I had gone skiing only a few times, but my brother wanted to take me on my first ski trip. He bought me my first pair of skis, a pair of K2s with Mickey Mouse on them. The ski trip my brother had planned was in northern Minnesota at Lutsen Mountain—an improvement over Mount Kato, but still not much.

G.P. was planning on taking his ex-girlfriend, Vicky, on the trip, so I was allowed to bring a friend myself. I decided to take my friend Barrett. We were pretty close, mainly because our parents forced us to go to church together, and we always hated church. So to blow time and make it through the service, the two of us hung out in the back pew and played with G.I. Joes.

I had some experience skiing, but not a lot. It was still more than Barrett, though. I don't remember a whole lot from the trip, other than it was cold and I caught a little air for the first time. But this was just the beginning of my love of snow sports.

Summer came around, and it was back to the usual all-day, every-day at the lake. Now I was inviting more and more friends to come out to the cabin. My circle of friends was starting to grow. All of my classmates were starting to become closer, too. With all our toys and lack of supervision, our cabin became the new hangout. My friends and I saw it as the perfect opportunity to throw our first party, and we decided to make it a big one.

My parents and brother were all willing to help out. We didn't plan on drinking, so that wasn't an issue, but we were still a bunch of crazy kids. My brother volunteered to chaperon. He had a nice stereo system to set up for the music. We also hauled in a dump truck of white sand so we could set up a volleyball court and a little beach area. We even set up an outdoor dance floor. We had water balloon launchers, a fire pit, and plenty of food. We were ready for the best party a middle-schooler could ever have. A party just to bring people together.

This would be the beginning of my addiction to and love of catering for others. I loved being the host and having happy guests. The party influenced me to start a DJing business with my friend, Marc. We threw numerous parties all over town at places like the American Legion, and we started DJing school dances. After helping Marc and his dad remodel and insulate their garage, we found it perfect to host more parties. We always had a good turnout.

By the following Christmas, I received my first snowboard, a Burton Cruise 135, from my brother. I had previously been riding a two-inch-thick, plastic Mogul Monster. However, my brother knew what was up and that I needed a real snowboard. Plastic snowboards were not allowed at ski resorts. In fact, resorts still required safety leashes be attached to your ankles. Resorts were also checking to make sure your snowboard had a metal edge, and my Mogul Monster was all plastic.

When I began this renegade sport, many resorts were still not allowing snowboards on them at all. We were all just misfits. I had been a skateboarder for several years by now, so I was already comfortable with this sort of harassment. I was now just a misfit on snow instead of concrete.

This year, my brother had another ski trip planned for me. This time, we were going to Indianhead Mountain on the northern peninsula of Michigan. My brother took his new girlfriend, Amy, on this trip so I took Barrett again. On our way to the resort, I was asleep in the back of Amy's Jeep Grand Cherokee. Suddenly, I woke up. We were spinning out of control. We had hit a patch of ice. Miraculously, we were still on the road and hadn't been hit by any oncoming traffic. It was my first near car accident, and we had pulled it off without a single scratch. It must have been fate, but it freaked me out. My heart was racing.

We made it safely to Indianhead. After checking into the condo and settling in, my brother informed us he had bought us some tubes. It was probably eleven or so at night, nice and dark out, and he had a great idea for us to go tubing down the bottom part of the ski slope. I later learned this was an extremely dangerous idea, but on this night, everything went well. A nice, bright orange plastic fence lined the bottom of the slope. So while we were sliding uncontrollably down the hill, we at least had the comfort of knowing there was a fence at the bottom to abruptly stop us.

During this trip, my brother decided to take Amy out to dinner, leaving me and Barrett unsupervised in the room. While they were out, we decided to have a surprise waiting for them when they came back. We were initially thinking something celebratory, like decorating. But we instead ended up doing what kids do: We trashed the room. We started making forts with the mattresses, and it looked like a party kids would enjoy. It was not what my brother or Amy expected when they came back from dinner.

By eighth grade, I had grown a little bit, so my brother upgraded me to a Burton Air 5.0, and he was planning our biggest trip yet. This was the trip that undoubtedly changed my life. The Christmas of '92, my brother wanted to take me to Vail, Colorado, for the first time. A ski resort before even becoming a town, Vail was a relatively young mountain, having only been founded twenty-nine years earlier. Vail was one of the first resorts in the country to fully embrace snowboarding. Most of the contests I watched on TV were held at Vail. As long as I had my steel edges and a leash on my ankle, I had full access to the mountain.

It was my first gondola ride, too. I waited in line on this long set of cheese-grater-like stairs. At the top, a small, metal box awaited. I had to carry my snowboard inside the tiny car. They had yet to design a snowboard rack for the outside, where the skis were traditionally held. On the ride up, I was amazed by the sheer size of the place; the length of the run and the expanse of mountains seemed endless. Underneath the gondola was a wide-open, groomed run. I watched a snowboarder carve perfectly laid-out turns completely perpendicular to the ground. The sight was amazing. What I zoned in on was, though, was that his board was shaped differently, and he was wearing what looked to be ski boots. He was riding what I later learned was simply called a race setup: a skinnier board with an offset side cut, fully directional.

One day, we were riding along this cat track through the trees where they had a little bobsled run for kids. The bobsled was essentially a large, padded box going down a short, curvy track on a mellow slope. It was cool to see, because I had always been fascinated with the Olympics. But something else nearby was what I was most interested in. It didn't look like much at the time and was far from rideable, but the snowboard half-pipe was located right there. During this time, pipe dragons didn't exist and the half-pipes were dug out by hand. Since there were no half-pipe contests on the schedule, the half-pipe was full of snow and all I could see was the general shape. But I was enthralled by the nostalgia of seeing it, thinking of all the pros who had once ridden there. This was huge for a kid from a tiny Minnesotan farm town. Watching contests on TV just didn't compare to seeing the location in person. I had imagined myself at a pro contest, feeling the energy and excitement. Now I was actually there. But there was no energy. I felt like I'd missed the party

Vail was having a good snow year. Having never been out West before, I assumed it was always like this in Colorado. On this trip, I even dropped my first cliff, albeit unintentionally. We were riding out in China Bowl, a wide open bowl-shaped oasis on the backside of Vail Mountain, during complete white-out conditions. I missed the large black signs that said, "Warning: Cliffs ahead," which were clearly posted with plenty of time to change course. I might have been a little too anxious and a little too eager for my first real powder turns. Besides, coming from Minnesota, I had never seen cliffs within skiable terrain before. So I took off ahead of the group, and just like that, I dropped my first cliff.

It was a series of cliffs known as Dragon's Teeth. I found myself completely buried in snow up to my neck. I was stuck. I didn't know it at the time, but Dragon's Teeth are far from the best cliffs to be dropping, as the landing is flat and the run-out even flatter. My brother spent a good portion of the day pulling me across this large, flat section of open space.

Other than getting stuck, I couldn't imagine snowboarding getting any better than Vail. The place was absolutely magical. I also was introduced to tree riding. The trees on the mountain were spaced out perfectly. As long as I was in some sort of control, I could always find fresh powder. Riding in powder was new to me, too. The Midwest was cold but rarely snowed more than a few inches, and all I really knew was groomed runs. In Vail, I learned what floating on a bed of air felt like. Nothing could compare to it.

During our visit to Colorado, my brother decided to take us on a road trip down to Boulder and check out the University of Colorado campus. We figured I would possibly go to school there someday, and it was never too early to think about my future. The campus was beautiful, and the buildings were all made of stone—but refined. It was a cross between a city and a mountain. It was amazing. From a distance, I could even see the Boulder Reservoir, so I felt if I chose to move there, I could still enjoy my water sports.

I made it back to Vail, and that's when I had my first ski bunny experience. I spotted a cute girl a little older than I was sitting at the base of the mountain. She was probably just mesmerized by my snowboard and had never seen one before. But she was cute and couldn't take her eyes off me. I naturally assumed she was checking me out, but I didn't have the guts to talk to her. If I hadn't already been in love with Vail, she sealed the deal for me.

The drive back to Minnesota was one of the longest drives of my life. I didn't want to leave. With the amazingly picturesque drive back over Vail Pass, I couldn't resist taking an enormous amount of scenic pictures. I had fallen in love with the mountains.

# Chapter: 3

## No Strings

The skateboarding scene was dying down, not just in my small farm town but in the entire country. I was losing interest, too, so I decided not to continue as an outcast. Marc and I were still DJing school dances and spending time out at the lake. We were desperately trying to hang onto what I consider the greatest memories of my childhood. I still dreamed of being a Jet Ski racer to feed my love for speed. The lake was my passion.

By 1992, I made the big jump to high school. I didn't want to be seen as a little kid anymore. However, as a freshman, I was the baby of the school. Freshman year was a blur. I was a confused kid, and I was starting to feel the effects of growing up. I could no longer get by with childhood innocence—not that I was that innocent—but I thought I was ready to grow up. With skateboarding becoming a fad, I looked for a new sport. I took up in-line skating, which was, after all, invented in Minnesota. This, just like the rest of high school, wasn't my finest moment. I was an average kid in pretty much every way possible: average grades in class and average outside of class. I tried not to stand out in school.

In-line skating was simple. It seemed like anyone could do it; the damn things are attached to you. I might as well have been an extreme alternative walker. Regardless, it was still fun jumping down stairs, spinning every which way, or even skating onto rails. In-line skating also made the ramps I had previously built still useful. I frequently skated up the hill toward my house, past the high school athletic fields. Many of the coaches saw me and tried to encourage me to join one of the teams. They thought I must be in good shape, and I also showed good athleticism in gym class. One day, I finally caved and joined the football team. I made it two weeks and decided it was one of the stupidest ideas I'd ever had. Organized sports were not for me, mostly because I lacked the kind of discipline needed to show up every day. Having to show up to school was difficult enough.

Every year, my brother continued taking me out west on ski trips; Minnesota no longer could compare. It was all about the snow. By the time I was in high school, we realized that Presidents' Day weekend in February was the best time for consistently good snow. From there forward, that was when we would plan our trips.

Throughout high school, my brother took me to Steamboat, Aspen, Jackson Hole, and four more mountains in Utah. Snowboarding was becoming my life. During this time, I kept thinking of that carving snowboarder I had seen cruising down Vail Mountain underneath the gondola, and I decided to get myself a carving board, too. I got a Burton M 6.1—not a full-blown race set-up, but it still had the asymmetrical shape with the offset side cut and a stiff flex.

Sophomore year came around, and it was time to finally get my driver's license. At the time, it was the greatest moment of my life. I easily passed my driving test, and as a present, my parents bought me a slightly used, year-old Ford Mustang convertible. It was candy apple red with a black top. I loved that car. Convertibles, in general, always exemplified the feeling of freedom. The fresh air and lack of confinement was what I really wanted.

Now that I finally had a driver's license and a car, I was no longer limited to my tiny hometown of Jackson. My brother had introduced me to life outside of this little bubble, and I wanted to explore more. Sometimes, I drove for hours with no real destination. I put a song on repeat and completely zoned out. Owning a car gave me my own private world. I had always felt like I was a bit of an outcast, and now nobody had to come with me.

My friends and I became more familiar with alcohol, and the parties out at the cabin were becoming more interesting. They were typical high-school parties: a bunch of teens hanging around, playing cards, and drinking. Eventually, we would get drunk enough to do stupid things, like shooting fireworks at each other and going skinny-dipping. I bought a pair of Cerwin Vega fifteen-inch speakers that really thumped. I loved throwing parties, but honestly, what I really liked was entertaining people.

My high-school parties were considerably smaller than the ones Marc and I threw in middle school, but there were always the usual suspects. Underage drinking was just accepted in our small farm town. Everyone (including my parents) knew I threw these parties, and it was a guarantee that the cops were going to show up. Every time the cops appeared, we sent the same friend out to go talk to them: Shawn. He seemed to know exactly how to deal with them.

Everyone else ran, including me. As it was my house, I probably should have been the one who stayed. But from my previous experiences with cops, I didn't trust them. Besides, running from cops was fun; it was always one hell of an adrenaline rush. As Shawn occupied the cops with god knows what kind of B.S., the rest of us ran a few cabins down and hid under a dock in the lake. No way they could find us. Not that they ever even bothered looking.

These cabin parties continued until I finally left town for good, but throughout high school, these were not my only parties. Now that I finally had a driver's license, all I really wanted to do was leave town. So every year on my birthday in March, I drove up to Minneapolis with as many friends as I could round up to celebrate. My brother, who had been living in the Twin Cities since he left for college a decade earlier, checked us into an Embassy Suites hotel and bought us booze, as long as we promised not to drive. Not driving? Not a problem. Being a small-town kid driving drunk in a city where I didn't know my way around didn't sound appealing to me. Not to mention I already hated drunk driving. A few years earlier, my good friend's sister had died in a drunk-driving accident.

My birthdays weren't the only excuse we needed to head to the cities for a weekend of fun. There were also state sporting events. The situation was the same: My brother checked us into a hotel, bought us booze, and we promised not to drive. State sporting events were amazing, because we were not alone and could socialize with other teens our age. The hotels were full of high-school kids, and the parties got crazier. On one of the trips, the drinking might have gotten a little out of control; we literally had to check out of the hotel, because someone had vomited in every sink in the room, and we couldn't handle the smell. I feel sorry for the housekeepers who had to clean up that mess.

Finally graduation arrived. The ceremony itself meant very little to me. I had been cruising through high school with average grades, because I was barely trying. The truth was, I hated school and it wasn't much of a challenge. So graduation wasn't much of a celebration of accomplishment, but rather a celebration of finally being allowed to leave town.

The summer after graduation was by far the wildest, and the cabin parties were frequent. I even reacquainted with my old friend, Matches. Being a few years older, he became our booze buyer. And if we weren't having parties at the cabin, we were still pulling all-nighters in random parks or simply walking the streets. One night, we were bored, so I decided to take a quick road trip to Wisconsin. It was a little over a three-hour drive, and we pulled into a grocery store in La Crosse. I stumbled out of the car like an eighteen-year-old kid who had just pulled an all-nighter. Which I was.

I walked up to the clerk and said, "I heard you have good cheese here in Wisconsin."

I bought some cheese, and we left. Our sole purpose for driving to Wisconsin was boredom and cheese.

This wasn't our first (or last) random road trip, either. One day, we drove all the way to Canada to drink. The legal age there was nineteen, and we thought it would be fun to experience alcohol legally. It was. Upon our arrival in Thunderbay, a cab driver directed us to the nastiest strip club I could have ever imagined, Centerfolds. After another night of vomiting, we headed back across the border for the seven-hour-drive back to Minneapolis.

During this time, I also made frequent trips down to Spirit Lake and Okoboji, Iowa, mostly because a recent Playboy article had called it one of the best places in the country to get laid. Okoboji was only a thirty-minute drive from Jackson, and it was a huge party town in the summer. The main strip was loaded with eighteen-and-older dance clubs and strip clubs, the typical things you would expect from a summer vacation spot. We were essentially a group of eighteen-year-old guys looking for chicks. And we found them. Two girls in particular. My friend, Jesse, met his future wife, Mindy, and I met my very brief summer fling, Coral.

Mindy's dad owned a chain of Godfather's Pizza shops and owned a beautiful house right on the lake. Jesse and I spent many nights hanging out at Mindy's. We also took Mindy and Coral down to my cabin for parties. Coral was working at a Jet Ski rental place at the time. Just like me, she had taken several trips out west to ski. Coral was quite possibly perfect for me, but the timing wasn't right.

I felt bad about how things ended between Coral and I, but just like every girl after her would learn, I was a tough person to date. Coral was a couple years younger than I was, and at the time, my dream was simple: I just didn't want to get locked down to this small farm town. I wanted to cut any sort of attachment that would hold me back.

***

When it was time for college, I chose the University of Minnesota, quite possibly because I wanted to follow in my brother's footsteps. I still had no clue what I was planning to do with my life, and I decided to simply do what was expected of me. I never even gave it a second thought. Filipinos valued higher education, and in my family, I didn't feel like I had a choice.

So, I signed up for general classes with no declared major. I moved to Minneapolis and into the dorms. My roommate was from Green Bay, a huge Packers fan. His parents owned the Kohler toilet manufacturing company. While I was living with him, he decided to join a fraternity. Through him, I made it to a few college parties, and I absolutely hated them. It felt like most of the kids had been raised with a far more sheltered life than I had lived. I felt the parties should have been far more "adult." I'm guessing a lot of it had to do with them being frat parties—and I knew I didn't belong.

My friend, Matt, who I had grown up skateboarding with in Jackson, was living in Minneapolis at the time, as well. Matt wasn't attending school at the time and was working at a clothing store. Some of his friends were planning a ski trip to Aspen, Colorado. It was an organized club trip of some sort. I didn't know the details exactly, but it didn't matter; we basically invited ourselves, packed up his little Honda, and made the twenty-hour journey through a blizzard in the middle of the night.

We made it to Aspen sometime in the morning and tried to get a little sleep in his car. Finally, we felt it was the appropriate time of day to knock on the condo door. The condo was really nice: the standard ski town type of wooden cabin with a large fireplace in the living room. The cabin was pretty cramped for the amount of people on the trip, so everyone claimed their floor space to sleep on. This was my first trip without the "parental guidance" of my brother, and it turned out to be a stereotypical college ski trip—an awesome party. As a thank you, Matt and I cooked a feast of spaghetti for the whole crew.

While at the University of Minnesota, my other friend, Mike, was going to St. Cloud State University, about an hour northwest of Minneapolis. One day, he invited my friend, Josh, and I up for a visit. We took the short trip north and were greeted by an amazing group of people. Mike was surrounded by a far better group of friends than I had been able to find at the U of M.

I still hated school. I quickly found myself on academic probation; I was doing well in classes that consisted of math and logic, such as economics, but completely bombing others. Although, ironically, I met the daughter of my economics teacher on one of my visits to St. Cloud. Maybe that helped with my grade. I could tell he at least liked me. The truth was, I still wasn't trying or putting forth any effort in school.

Over Christmas break, our newly made friends from St. Cloud State invited us to a party at their home in Minnetonka. It was a nice, more mature type of party. Nothing like the wild and crazy college parties I had been used to, and I liked that.

During this party, I met an amazing girl named Amy. She was attending college in Lynchburg, Virginia—not exactly close to Minneapolis. Amy and I were up all night talking. We became pen pals via email. (Yes, we finally had the internet!) I found Amy intriguing; she seemed more intellectual than most of my friends. Part of what I liked was that she went to school far away from her home state of Minnesota. She wasn't afraid of being far from her friends and family. Amy was the first person I'd ever met who had left family and friends behind to do her thing. I had even chosen the University of Minnesota because it was close to home. Amy was a year older than me, and having already spent a year out in Lynchburg, she seemed to be doing well.

Once school was out for the summer, I could move out of the dorms. I still had absolutely no desire to move back home to Jackson, so I moved in with my old friend, Gunner, who had been living in nearby Shakopee. He was attending a school for architecture, a job I felt he would have been great at.

Gunner's roommate happened to be working at a nearby amusement park called Valleyfair. I needed a job, so after he told me they were hiring, I turned in an application. I knew I couldn't waste another summer hanging out at the lake, so I accepted a position on the bathroom crew. Before you disregard the position as a disgusting, low-level position, I was most proud of this job. At a whopping $6 per hour, we were the highest-paid employees at the park. On top of that, we got to roam around the park all day long. Since they needed someone to check both the men's and women's rooms, we were always paired up with someone of the opposite sex. It was a great summer job, and it was the beginning of my understanding of "work family."

We started what we called "Valley-affairs." Yes, the typical hookups in the workplace. At work, I was called Brother Paul. There was Brother Brent, Sister Kara, and so on; we were family and continued to remain close long after we left. Valleyfair had fun benefits, like Ride Night or Water Park Night, when the park was open for employees only. After work, the crew spent late nights together, often ending up at my nearby apartment or at a twenty-four-hour Perkins drinking coffee. The servers must have hated us. We stayed there for hours drinking bottomless coffee.

While living with Gunner, I taught myself how to gamble and win at blackjack. Our apartment was only a five-minute drive from the Mystic Lake Casino, where the gambling age was only eighteen. So nearly every night that the crew didn't feel like hanging out, I took twenty dollars and played blackjack. If I doubled the twenty dollars, I would walk away. If I lost it, I was done. I had discipline. I always kept my winnings in a separate stash from the rest of my money, so eventually I was playing with the house's money. My gambling profits made it up to a thousand dollars, at which point I decided to try my luck again. This time, I took the full grand using the same strategy: double it or lose it all and walk away. I lost it all. Though I have been to casinos many times since, it still stands as my largest one-night loss.

During this summer, a local radio station decided to have a large music festival originally called Edgefest (later known as X-Fest). The festival was held just across the border in Wisconsin. My Valleyfair crew decided to plan a short road trip to the show. Still underage, we knew we wouldn't be able to drink at the festival. So, we did the typical pre-partying: drinking a few forties of malt liquor so we could get a good buzz going. Not surprisingly, while we were stuck in a long line of traffic, I had to relieve myself. I jumped out of the car and ran behind a house, whipped it out, and let it go. Next thing I knew, an old, long-haired hippie in a tie-dyed shirt came running out of the house after me. It looked like he was about to tackle me. When he got to about five feet away, he realized what I was doing, and he quickly stopped and jumped back.

"Whoa, whoa!" he said. "Hey, next time, just knock on the door."

That was that. We went on our way.

Once we made it to the festival, we had to stand in another long line to get in. In line, we passed a bottle of whiskey around; we figured it would be our last taste of alcohol until after the show. There was no way we were sneaking booze past security, and we wouldn't be able to buy beer once we were in.

It rained a lot during the show, and it was muddy. A good-sized mosh pit was developing. It was a pit of mud, and as usual, most guys were much bigger than I was, but it didn't matter. No one could get any footing in the mud, and everyone was covered. I'd never considered myself the "mosh-pit type," but I figured what the hell, and I jumped in the pit.

During the show, I also witnessed crowd-surfing for the first time. I had grown up watching the music videos of the glam bands, and I had always idolized the amount of fun they showed on stage. Stage-diving, they were the epitome of larger than life. Now I was witnessing it in person, and I had to try it. This was where being a "little guy" helped, as I asked some guys to hoist me up. Next thing I knew, I was being grabbed everywhere, private places included, by random strangers. I was able to float over the crowd for the duration of full songs. I now fully understood why it was known as "crowd-surfing." The feeling of floating was amazing.

Amy was back from school in Lynchburg and was spending her summer at her parents' house on Lake Minnetonka. After emailing each other throughout the school year, we had become good friends. I found myself spending quite a bit of time at her parents' house, and her parents seemed to like me, too, which was a bonus. What I liked most about her house was that it was right on the lake. We could easily walk to numerous public beaches from her house.

I was hanging out at Amy's one day, and she introduced me to her friend, Becky. Becky was a short, little, blond bombshell, the type of girl you would see and completely lose your train of thought. She was stunningly beautiful. Just like Amy, I found Becky to be extremely intellectual. As it turned out, opposites really did attract, considering I never thought of myself as intellectual. Becky became my summer-long fling. Although it was just a fling, the summer with Becky was the most romantic relationship of my life. We spent late nights hanging out on the beaches of Lake Minnetonka; that was all we really needed. But unfortunately, that was it. It was just a fling. She eventually left to go back to school, and I never saw her again.

Once summer was over, it was time for me to go back to school. This time, I avoided the dorms and got an apartment with my sister's boyfriend, who lived just across the river from campus. The living situation was miles better than the dorm. However, I still hated school. No longer living in the dorms, I had no problem avoiding the crappy frat parties that had made my freshman year possibly the worst time of my life. But the new living situation was not helping my grades. I still wasn't focused enough to pay any sort of attention in class and was still taking many trips up north to St. Cloud State. Mike's group of friends were quickly becoming my group of friends, as well. In Minne-apolis, I was still struggling to make any of my own real friends. I didn't fit in.

Over Christmas break, I decided to plan a ski trip back up to Lutsen, this time inviting Mike, my friend Josh, and a few of our friends from St. Cloud State. I planned the whole trip. I even booked a nice ski-in/ski-out condo with a hot tub. I wanted to do it right, like the trips my brother took me on as a kid. Regardless of the skiing, it was an adventure, starting with me forgetting to close the ski rack on the top of the car. My snowboard ended up in the middle of the gravel road. I may have not been surrounded by the most hard-core of skiers, but it didn't matter. The ski town vibe was what I liked. The atmosphere of a winter wonderland.

After the break, I returned back to school. Well, sort of. Phys-ically, I was there, but mentally, I was somewhere completely different.

One day, I was hanging out at a local snowboard shop, flirt-ing with the cute sales clerk. In addition to giving me good deals on gear, she told me about a snowboard park at nearby Highland Hills and how they never checked lift tickets. You accessed the snowboard park via a rope tow, so the resort figured there was no need to pay a lift operator to stand there and watch people grab the rope. Back in the day, my brother had taken me there—to what was the coolest half-pipe contest I had ever seen. The half-pipe went the entire length of the run, but to top it off, it had an elbow halfway down the pipe. The riders could incorporate a hip transfer in the middle of their runs. I also remember witnessing girls practicing hand plants at the bottom of the pipe. They didn't dig half-pipes like that anymore.

So, I was intrigued by the opportunity to snowboard for free, no season pass required. This was the beginning of the end of my days at the University of Minnesota. I now skipped classes on a regular basis. One day I outshot a jump and landed flat. I never went to the doctor, but I could tell something wasn't right. I presumably had just broken my tailbone. I knew there was not much a doctor could do, so I just toughened up and tried to return to class.

Shortly thereafter, I had a lecture to go to. All the lecture halls at the university were set up like large auditoriums with old, wooden bucket seats—those wooden seats that were carefully carved out to perfectly fit your butt. Those seats had a mound in the center to perfectly conform to your ass, but not exactly what you want with a broken tailbone. I thought I could sit through the lecture on a couple thick, well-insulated jackets for padding. I was wrong. I probably needed a doughnut with a hole in the middle. Either way, that lecture effectively ended my time not only at the University of Minnesota, but in the Midwest in general. I knew I had to move to Colorado. I was done with the ice of the Midwest.

I needed powder.

# Chapter 4:

## Searching for Direction

I was perplexed on what to do next. All I knew was that I wouldn't be going back to the University of Minnesota. By this time, my old friend, Marc, from my DJing days, had moved up to the cities. Without college, he had landed some sort of well-paying computer job. Marc's younger brother, Brad, had also moved into town. The old, good-times crew was finally back together.

This turned out to be another rowdy summer, as Marc and I traveled to house parties all over the state of Minnesota. Marc even began dating a girl from a small town in northern Minnesota who would later become the mother of his first child. Brad got me a job at a local car rental place, so I was at least making a little money. Money was all the job was good for. I didn't learn any skills or life experiences.

By this time, we had friends all over the state and regularly hung out at house parties. I kept close contact with my old Valleyfair family. Sister Kara was attending the U of M and was living in a party house off campus. She had quite a few roommates, and there always seemed to be something going on there. The whole crew was into live music. They threw a lot of parties and met a lot of local bands. I also found myself going to quite a few shows. I had a good group of friends around the Minneapolis area, but by now my range of friends around the country interested me more.

Amy had decided to stay in Virginia for the summer. At the same time, Marc had a business trip to Washington, D.C., so I figured it was a good time for a road trip. Sister Kara and Brother Brent were both down, so we loaded in my cozy, little Mustang, and we hit the road. The three of us went on an adventure halfway across the country.

Our first stop was Chicago, and we were greeted with rush-hour traffic. It didn't take us long before we were already lost, so we pulled over at a gas station, letting the traffic clear out a bit. Finally back in the car, we were able to check out the city. We walked down along a pier on Lake Michigan, and I instantly could tell why it was named the Windy City. Driving around the city in the middle of the night, we passed through what was the sketchiest neighborhood I had ever been in, somewhere around Chinatown. We locked the doors and wanted to get the hell out of there.

Our next stop was Washington, D.C., another twelve hours away. When we pulled into D.C., we found ourselves in a neighborhood quite similar to the one we had left in Chicago. I was beginning to learn how sheltered I had really been. Whether I had been born in Jackson or Minneapolis, it was still the Midwest. I probably shouldn't have been as nervous as I was, but we were all still young and a long way from our comfort zone. After driving around the city for a while, we made it to Marc's hotel. His work had put him up with a pretty nice suite. Our entire time in D.C. was mainly spent at the hotel, partly because new cities scared me at the time. Not to mention we weren't of the drinking age yet, so there was not much for us to do anyway. By the morning, we were on our way to Lynchburg.

In Lynchburg, I was reunited with Amy. She gave us a quick tour of the campus and from there, she drove us up the Appalachian Mountains. The Appalachians were nothing like the Rockies. They were green and more reminiscent of rolling hills. I was not blown away by the sheer size of the mountains, like I had been in Colorado, but it was the pure beauty of forests— it was majestic. Amy, as expected, was a knowledgeable host. She shared stories of the area and gave us a good history lesson. As the sun began to go down in the mountains and the dark began to set in, the stories transitioned into ghost stories. The night turned into another memorable evening in the mountains.

Amy had a nice apartment off campus with a pool. I have an image engraved in my mind of Brother Brent doggy paddling across the pool with a rose in his mouth. Brent had never learned to swim, nor was he the most athletic or coordinated of people, so it was a sight to take in and remember. As he not-so-gracefully delivered the rose to Amy, it was comical, to say the least.

Around Halloween, Marc brought up the fact that his cousin, Shirola, was living in Aurora, a suburb of Denver in Colorado. As was clear by now, I was all about the spontaneous trips. So, of course, we loaded up the car and off we went. This was the one and only time I ever met Shirola, and she was another hottie. I honestly think Marc might have been trying to hook me up with his cousin. She threw a little house party, things got a little blurry. Marc and I somehow got separated, I woke up on Shirola's floor. Marc found himself waking up in a random house at another party down the street. He asked around if anyone knew who his cousin was, because he was lost.

The next day, I woke up and took a drive up the mountains to the nearest ski hill. Loveland Ski Area was about an hour away.

I bought a relatively cheap ticket, as it was preseason and very few runs were open. After snowboarding all day, I was leaving and saw a sign posted for snowboard instructors wanted. I asked to meet with the supervisor. After a quick chat with him, I asked what the qualifications were to be an instructor.

His response: "Can you stand up on a green and speak in complete sentences?"

After watching the movie Aspen Extreme, I was expecting more. Shocked by his passive response, I answered with a quick, "Yes." And just like that, I had a job before even moving to Colorado.

Back in Minnesota came the tricky part: How to tell my parents I was moving to Colorado? My solution was simple. Just don't tell them. I let my sister do the dirty work, which I assumed went something like, "Hey, Mom. Paul's moving to Colorado." At age twenty, I was somewhat of an adult at this point, and I was making my own decisions. I somehow talked my sister into driving to Colorado with me to help me find an apartment over Thanksgiving break. I didn't think my parents were quite ready for me to completely drop out of school, so I enrolled at the University of Colorado at Boulder. After finding an apartment, I packed up my car and began the long drive by myself to Boulder.

Upon arriving, I found myself back at the campus that my brother had showed me many years earlier. Boulder was exactly how I remembered it: a cross between a city and a mountain town. However, I wasn't the same twelve-year-old little kid. I remember Christmas being the saddest and most depressing experience of my life. I was never really close with my roommate, nor can I even remember his name. So when he left to spend the holidays with his family somewhere nearby, I was by myself in our empty apartment. I was alone for the holidays for the first time ever. I was lonely, near tears. I had been in Colorado for a mere month, so I knew no one. For the Christmas of '98, I sat alone in an empty apartment, no Christmas tree and no presents, not even any phone calls. I felt disconnected and forgotten, and it hurt. It made me question my choice to leave my world behind to start somewhere new.

School started, but I wasn't doing very well at it. All I was working toward was just getting by. However, I do remember getting my first ever A in a college course. It was a writing class with a relatively young, good-looking instructor. A paper I particularly remember her liking was something about gang violence and the death of Tupac Shakur.

I was making a few friends in school this time, and I was actually somewhat having fun. I had classmates I could study with, and we helped each other out. The truth was, I felt like I could achieve a degree—if only I knew what that degree should be. Once, I trekked through a full-blown flash flood just to get to a study group. I walked through a tunnel filled with two feet of rushing water, through pouring rain while soaking wet, and that didn't even stop me. I had more determination than when I was attending the University of Minnesota. However, I had no clear goals when it came to school. I was still searching for some sort of direction in life.

On weekends, I made the hour-long drive up to Loveland Ski Area, where I was a snowboard instructor. I developed new work friends. Now, these were the type of friends I could relate to. They were at least snowboarders. I met a fun married couple, Joe and Shannon, who recently relocated from Illinois. Joe and Shannon quickly became my best friends and made me feel comfortable in my new home of Colorado. We shared the same passion for snowboarding. What opened my mind the most about this couple were their unconventional wedding rings: They were tattooed on their fingers rather than a piece of expensive metal—and I loved that. They thought outside the box, and I considered the tattoos as revolutionary.

Joe and Shannon lived in Denver, only a thirty-minute drive from Boulder. Whenever we had the opportunity to go snowboarding, we carpooled up to the mountains. One day in late February, peak season, Joe and I went riding at Winter Park. It would have been an amazing powder day, as the snow was heavily falling from the sky. I say "would have been," because on our very first run, I chose to take a trip through the terrain park. As a twenty-year-old, I was always riding balls to the wall, not bothering to feel things out. I went straight toward the first jump and then blacked out. To this day, I don't really know what had happened. Joe didn't see it happen, either. I somehow knocked myself unconscious. I came to, and I couldn't move my shoulder.

Regardless, I was determined to make it down the mountain. After painfully getting to the bottom, or at least what I thought was the bottom, there was nowhere to go. We weren't back to the parking lot, but rather on another section of the mountain requiring us to take a lift back up. At this point, I knew I could no longer snowboard. I was in pain.

Joe called ski patrol, and I was off and onto my first and only ever toboggan ride. Ski patrol took me to the first-aid room, and after X-rays, I was diagnosed with a separated shoulder. I had torn the ligament holding my collarbone down. I also probably had a concussion, as I couldn't remember a thing. The doctor gave me some pain pills, and I was on my way.

The drive home was also a bit of a blur; I guess drugs and a hatred for what had just happened will do that. I have a tendency to forget about the bad moments in life and always move forward. I remember Joe giving me a hit of his pot pipe. I'd never been much of a weed aficionado, but it was my favorite pain killer. I also remember it was a major blizzard and was dumping snow all the way down the mountains into Boulder. Something stressful happened on the ride back. I was too high off weed and hopped up on Percocet to remember for sure, but I think we got stuck in a ditch or something. Either way, we made it.

The injury ultimately ended my career as a snowboard instructor. Even once my shoulder healed, I never returned to work. The season was nearly over. Back in Boulder, I had other friends, but none of them meant very much to me. I simply didn't belong in Boulder. I didn't belong in school.

As a result of not knowing where else to go, I found myself going back to more frat parties. I hated frat parties. Why was I there? I simply couldn't sit still. So, I went to frat parties and raves with groups of guys who had probably been jocks in high school; this was not my kind of crowd. I was introduced to drugs like cocaine and ecstasy, pulling all-nighters and basically getting fucked up. Frat parties and raves were not my thing, but I was a young guy willing to give anything a shot.

During this time, I also became good friends with some guys who lived in the apartment one level below my place. They were a couple of outcasts themselves, motorcycle guys. I could relate to them better than the "jocks." They were the type of people who seemed like they didn't get along with the "cool" crowd. The gearheads from high school who would clearly butt heads with the jocks or popular kids in school. I found them nonthreatening, and this resulted in a simple friendship. The friendship turned out to be instrumental in my future.

Once the lease for my apartment expired, I returned to Minnesota to regroup. During this let's-go-figure-out-my-life break, I spent some quality time with my old friends. I got to hang out with my good, ol' high school buddies and my Valleyfair family. Although I wasn't exactly sure of my plans, my biggest challenge to date was on my horizon.

I drove up to northern Minnesota and went on a little camping trip all by myself. I drove around and set up camp. The peaceful solitude of northern Minnesota is what I wanted. It was quite the change from my depressed loneliness when I first moved to Boulder over the holidays. That forced solitude ultimately helped me grow and adjust. Now, I sought out alone time as comfort. I was becoming more comfortable with being alone; the social kid who used to always be surrounded by friends was slowly evolving into an introvert. But my camping trip was short. I needed to find my new home.

So I drove my homeless ass back to Boulder. Very thankfully, my former, motorcycle-riding neighbors were willing to take me in, allowing me to sleep on their couch until I could find a new apartment in Vail. I knew my college days were officially completely over. I felt bad for wasting my parents' money on schooling. In fact, I still feel bad about it. Going to college was the only regret I ever had in my life.

While couch surfing at my old neighbors' apartment in Boulder, I made frequent trips up to Vail. I was looking for both jobs and housing; whichever came first didn't matter. However, the nearly two-hour drive from Boulder was taking its toll, and I felt I was outstaying my welcome. Eventually, my former neighbors kicked me out.

I was out on the streets, on my own, and homeless. I was a college dropout with virtually zero meaningful job experience, so no one would hire me. This was before cell phones, so even if a job wanted to hire me, it had no way of getting a hold of me. But with no "real" work experience and no proper education, job offers were certainly not knocking down my door. Partially because I had no door to knock on. I was fully homeless, with no friends to stay with and not even a couch to sleep on. I spent nights sleeping in my car, often looking for places where I could park without being hassled, usually high up a mountain pass. This was October in the Rockies, so nights were cold, to say the least.

To help with my personal hygiene and general well-being, I occasionally splurged for a hotel room, charged to my credit card. To save money, I often found myself driving hours away to the most economical motel I could find. I alternated between nights in my car and nights in a mediocre motel. My parents knew about my situation and tried to help however they could, but they weren't happy with my choice to move to Vail. Again, I was doing my own thing, and no one could stop me. They never stopped caring about me, but they could not control me.

In order to build a life in Vail, I knew I needed to actually be in Vail. So, one night I checked into the Roost Lodge, an economical, "budget" hotel in Vail. Luckily, it was in the off-season, or I couldn't have afforded even that. Vail was one of Colorado's most expensive places to live. Not only was I trying to make it on my own, but I was trying to make it in one of Colorado's most expensive cities. It was an ambitious and wild move. But I was all in.

I was sitting in the hot tub in the Roost Lodge one evening when I saw two guys walking off a Greyhound Bus. They had apparently just met each other, on a seemingly crappy bus ride. As I soaked in the hot tub, I overheard them talking about needing to find a place to live. Just like me, they had the aspiration of making Vail their new home.

On a whim, I chimed in, "Hey, I need a place to live, too."

They were friendly and intrigued. We went out for drinks, starting off at what was then called the Half Moon Saloon, a dive of a ski town bar and grill in West Vail. After a few drinks, we decided to check out Vail Village, so we walked out to the Frontage Road and stuck out our thumbs. This was the first time I had ever hitchhiked. A pickup truck pulled over, and the three of us jumped in the back.

Once in Vail Village, we went to the nearest bar, a dark pub located at the beginning of Bridge Street down a set of stairs. The bar, named The George,  had only been around for a year or two, but it already felt like a Vail staple. Sitting on some old, raggedy couches with a coffee table that had magazine cutouts laminated into the top, we discussed finding a living situation.

I learned that Reed, who we eventually nicknamed "Reeee-tard" (an inappropriate nickname in more ways than one), was from New York City and had worked on Wall Street making good money. Although Reed hated Wall Street, he was business-savvy (he would ultimately be honored as Colorado's small-business person of the year for his company, Ink Monstr). Other than his business knowledge, Reed was also a passionate snowboarder.

As for the other guy, well, I don't remember his name, because he didn't last long. He was nineteen years old and was just released from prison for theft. He grew up outside of Grand

Junction and told stories of always coming to Vail and stealing bikes. I didn't care about his criminal past; I was looking for a new household. My dream was to make Vail home. So, on this one night out, we decided the three of us would find a place to live together.

As we searched ads in the Vail Daily, the local newspaper, we found a four-bedroom home in a West Vail. The house was in a neighborhood called Matterhorn, on the south side of the highway just a couple miles down the road from Vail Village. It was part of a two-story, eight-bedroom house with each floor rented out as a separate unit. Since the apartment was four bedrooms, we need another roommate.

Just as I had landed a job a year earlier as a snowboard instructor, Reed soon was hired for the same position, although this time in Vail. (I didn't have the patience to return to teaching.) During a work gathering—a meeting of some sorts—Reed decided to stand up in front of the group and simply yell out, "Hey, does anyone here need a place to live?" A random girl, Abby, replied with, "Hey, I do!" And that was how we found our fourth roommate.

I referred to Abby as a "hippie." She liked letting her hair go, wore a lot of tie-dye, and loved Jimi Hendrix. Abby was also from Minnesota. She had attended the University of Minnesota and was on the ski team. Unlike me, though, she actually graduated. She never used her degree, or even cared to try. Abby openly admitted she was just there to race as a member of the U of M ski team.

With Abby on board, we responded to the ad, signed the lease, and that was that. Without my newfound housemates, I would have never been able to make my dream a reality. I was finally a resident of Vail, Colorado.

# Chapter 5:

## Bums and Proud

The young thief of a roommate lasted a mere month and was quickly replaced with a friend of a friend, Drunk Rob. Drunk Rob was a slightly older guy. He had been living in Vail a few years before my arrival. Hailing from southern California, as the nickname implied, he drank a lot.

Occupying the upstairs of the house were five guys who grew up together in Virginia just outside of Washington, D.C.; our neighbors sharing the same roof had moved in a month earlier. Regardless of the fact that the apartments were rented out separately, I still thought of all of us as roommates.

Everyone had a nickname. Upstairs, we had Evil Dave, Silly Billy, C.J. the Conceited Jerk, Fat Craig, and Tommy—I guess not everyone had a nickname. Tommy needed a nickname.

Downstairs, they called me Paul-Asian (I liked to shorten it into one word: Paulasian), Drunk Rob, Reeeedtard, and the hippie, Abby. We were essentially a household full of chuckleheads, but we were all in Vail for the same reason: the amazing mountain.

I found myself in an ideal situation, and I felt like I finally fit in. Rob and Abby were skiers, and the rest of us were hard-core snowboarders. We were snowboarders and skaters to the fullest. We rode our boards sixteen hours a day. Fitting into society meant nothing. We were bums and proud of it. We also had the perfect backyard. With a short hike from the top of a ski lift, we could ride all the way to our back door. Those chuckleheads upstairs even cut out a portion of the railing on their deck and built a ramp, so you could actually ride directly into their living room.

Tommy took a job managing the brand new "Burton Yurt" snowboard demo center on top of the mountain. Tommy's co-worker, Chris, managed the brand new N.T.C. High Performance ski demo center located halfway up the mountain at Mid-Vail. Chris needed help getting the shop open and offered me the job. I was paid $9 per hour for the first two weeks, and I worked roughly sixty hours a week. My first paycheck consisted of around forty hours of overtime pay, so I received a good-sized check.

With the shop not yet in functioning order (it was still being built), my job was to construct an elevated wooden ramp with a pit dug in the middle so our guests could just ski up. With the ramp, their bindings would be at the tech's eye level, so adjusting the bindings and DINs to the appropriate level would be easy. It would be a quick and convenient ski-in/ski-out shop. After finishing the construction of the tech center, we filled the yurt with skis, set up TVs (for watching ski videos), and hooked up a register. My first two weeks on the job were the hardest I would have to work. By the following pay period, I had been promoted to assistant manager and put on salary with an increase of pay to $10 per hour for forty hours per week. With the shop set up, my workweek would only average around thirty-six hours per week. So switching over from hourly to salary worked out well for me.

Now my job was a breeze, and our backyard was a snowboarder's paradise. We built our own personal terrain park, complete with a fun, little gap jump off a small cliff through some branches and a small flat section that you had to clear. We also set up a few rails and log slides, which we manufactured, but usually are natural features of fallen trees. This was a first for me and, as it turned out, for most people, as well. Using hand saws or even chainsaws, we cut down trees and dragged them down the mountain, a practice that is not only frowned upon but also illegal, as this was U.S. Forest land. Regardless, we hauled these logs to our backyard and cut them appropriately. We buried posts to hold up the logs in various positions, creating the shape of obstacle we were looking for. We went for shapes like rainbows or A-frames, a pyramid or a "C-bow." Whatever we felt would be fun, a little different.

We needed a way to ride our personal park at night, since most of us had day jobs or simply rode the mountain during operating hours. Our park needed lights. I drove down to nearby Avon with Evil Dave and Silly Billy to the nearest Walmart. After searching through halogen lamps and other various outdoor lighting, we came across these incredibly powerful mercury-vapor lamps. Mercury is a somewhat dangerous chemical element; it has been phased out in most practical purposes for its health and safety concerns. However, when used for light fixtures, it is damn near as bright as the sun. So after returning to our man-made park, we ghetto-mounted three mercury-vapor lamps to the trees in our backyard, then ran an extension cord through our kitchen window. We sacrificed the warmth of our home for light in our backyard. Plug in the cord, and we had daylight!

This winter, Evil Dave bought himself a cheap Honda CRV for around five hundred bucks. It was all dented up and spray-painted blue and black; it looked like the Boozman's car from Thrashin' before they cut the top off. Our neighbors' driveway butted up against our backyard and onto a perfect mound of dirt and snow approximately five feet high. So Evil Dave decided to have his car plowed sideways onto this mound and make it a new feature for our park. We built a perfect jump/hip combo on this mound and could air over his car or jib it for boardslides. Evil Dave's car was a great addition to our backyard.

One day, after a somewhat crappy day of work, I decided I wanted to huck my first ever backflip over the car. Evil Dave was there shaping the jump as I told him my idea.

He responded, "You probably want a little more kick?"

"Probably," I calmly responded as I hiked by with my snow-board. I think I would have tried it either way. I hiked as far as I could up the hill onto another neighbor's yard and charged toward the jump. With full commitment, I threw myself inverted, easily clearing over Evil Dave's heap of metal. I landed a little off axis, but I didn't land on my head. My first backflip was somewhat of a success. Becoming inverted was my new obsession.

I was sessioning the jump over Evil Dave's car one afternoon when our disgruntled neighbor came running out of his house, yelling at me. He threatened to call the cops. Since I was doing nothing wrong, I yelled back, "Go ahead. Call the cops!" Sure enough, a cop showed up and ran my ID. Drunk Rob, being drunk (of course), tried explaining to the cop that the neighbor was on his "second box of wine," and we should all ignore him. I don't think drunk Rob helped the situation. Suddenly, the cop pulled out the handcuffs. He secured them around my wrists and led me to the back of his Saab squad car.

I had a warrant out for my arrest. I had previously gotten a speeding ticket and went to court for it. This was my first and only time I had to deal with Judge Buck. Judge Buck was a well-known, local, kind-hearted judge. I received a measly hundred dollar fine. Since it was the holidays, as a portion of my fine, I was offered an option of donating a twenty-dollar gift to the Toys for Tots nonprofit. I accepted the offer and paid a fine of eighty dollars, with an agreement that I would donate a gift to Toys for Tots.

I procrastinated and neglected to buy the present, not taking the donation seriously; I didn't think much of it. Well, it turned out to be serious. The judge put out a warrant for my arrest. The possibility that I could have a warrant didn't cross my mind when I told the neighbor to call the cops. But now, I was under arrest. For forgetting to wrap up a cheap gift for Toys for Tots. While I was at the police station being fingerprinted, filling out paperwork, and being booked into jail, Drunk Rob showed up, kindly bailing me out after my brief time in custody. I thankfully didn't have to spend a single night in jail.

With my backyard arrest, the authortities were now aware of our private park, in addition to the illegally mounted mercury-vapor lamps. According to the authorities, the lamps needed to be hardwired and professionally mounted, complete with buried power cables. Apparently, our combination of duct tape, string, and an extension cord running through our window did not qualify as being "professional." We replaced the lights with a combination of halogen lamps and Christmas lights. Our backyard at least looked festive now.

Our house had also become known as a party house. Large backyard bonfires and local DJs made for good celebrations. At some point, our house had also become known as an illegal marijuana supplier. My housemates were all huge marijuana aficionados, and one of my housemates decided to convert his closet into a growing facility. After constructing a sealed wall of Sheetrock, the operation became well hidden. Still, at some point, the authorities became suspicious, and they raided our house. Luckily, just before the raid occurred, Evil Dave had become paranoid and dismantled the operation. When the police arrived to search our home, they found nothing left except the equipment. After a court appearance, a minor fifty-dollar fine was dealt out. We escaped any serious charges.

Our first winter, my housemates had also heard of an indoor mini ramp that was on a ranch in Carbondale, just outside of Aspen, a little more than an hour away. The ramp was free to the public; we just had to be courteous to the owners and turn off the lights when we left. So around ten or eleven at night, we would drive out to Carbondale and skate this nearly perfect indoor ramp until two or three in the morning. We often snowboarded all day, even riding our yard after the mountain closed. We would then head to Carbondale to skateboard until early in the morning and repeat the following day. That was our lives. We worked stress-free jobs and rode our boards just about every waking hour of the day.

When companies, such as Burton, improved the design and function of snowskates (the original ones were basically skateboard decks without trucks), we started sneaking them onto the mountain. Snowskates were still illegal at resorts, so we had to sneak them up in large duffle bags after hours. The gondola would run until ten at night to service the restaurant on the mountain and the ice-skating rink. Late nights after dark were the only time we could skate down the mountain. We occasionally used headlamps, but normally we just used the light of the moon. Nothing beats full-moon riding.

Springtime came around, and that was when I really wanted to snowboard. I had been working at the demo center taking two-hour ski breaks every day, mainly taking laps on the nearby Chair Four to maximize my time; dropping the "Hollywood Cliffs" were what my ski breaks consisted of. These Chair Four cliffs were directly under the chair and always had an audience, hence their name; with a crowd and the right tricks, you could become famous on the mountain. I wanted to "ride the mountain" and have more time to snowboard. I asked Chris to demote me, and I effectively became a part-timer. An Australian girl, who I admittedly didn't get along with very well, took my position as management.

In April, the legendary B.B. and B party was going on. B.B. and B. was a renegade, unsanctioned party that started in the sixties and was held on the second Tuesday of April every year. The ski shop was slow, as it was toward the end of the season, so I asked my newly promoted boss if I could go check out the party. She said sure and let me go. She apparently was expecting me to come back to close, but I didn't see it that way and didn't return. It was immature of me to leave thinking everything would be fine, so it should not have come as a surprise that she fired me.

My first B.B. and B. was a wild experience. B.B. and B stood for whatever you wanted it to: beer, buds, boomers, boobs, butts, and bikinis were popular options. The party was held in the middle of the dense woods. A Snowcat track ran directly through the middle. While everyone partied, three guys decided to bring an inflatable canoe up the mountain. Under the influence of drugs, alcohol, and bad judgment, they decided to attempt to ride the canoe down the mountain—ultimately running into a tree and becoming seriously injured. It was reminiscent of the time I rode tubes down the hill in Michigan and was abruptly stopped by a fence.

I also watched my then-boss, Chris, ski buck naked through the center of the party. After being bombarded with a barrage of snowballs, he made it to the center of the raucous crowd and got tackled—fully naked. I had just witnessed my boss be the craziest person at the party. If Chris was acting rowdy, I didn't feel bad for being part of the party, too. I couldn't help but feel like I got fired because that Aussie girl felt left out.

The following year, there was a massive police presence at the party, along with Snowcats shuttling down the partygoers. This year, I arrived to the celebration with an entire one-eighth ounce of psychedelic mushrooms. With the large police presence, I became nervous carrying around my bag of illegal drugs, so I decided to eat the entire bag all at once. If I didn't have anything on me, I figured I couldn't get into any trouble.

I had never tripped that hard in my entire life. I literally rolled around on the ground laughing for a full five hours. Still heavily under the influence of drugs, I managed to ride my snowboard safely to the base of the mountain. I opted not to take the safe Snowcat shuttle down. I believed that if you can't handle your drugs, you have no business taking them.

Little did I know, this would be my last taste of B. B. and B. The following year, the entire area was shut down weeks before the annual party was even scheduled—effectively shutting down the festival forever.

But that wasn't all. B. B and B. was held at Minnie's Deck, a hidden area in the woods and a total legacy. Minnie's Deck had long been a local hangout, as few tourists would venture that deep into the woods to find it. The deck was especially nice during springtime when the sun set much later in the day. Often, we gathered at the deck for our last run well past resort hours, waiting for the groomers and ski patrol to make their final sweeps. Ski patrol would check on us and simply say, "You guys are on your own." They trusted us to make it down the mountain safely. After the mountain closed, the few of us remaining often stayed late for the unmatched joy of riding a wide open, empty, freshly groomed face of corduroy. Although many events and many people who couldn't handle their drugs and alcohol could have ultimately ended Minnie Deck's existence, I still blame the three idiots riding an inflatable canoe and catching police attention at B. B. and B. Minnie's Deck was permanently shut down.

With the Vail "mud season" in full effect, I was officially out of job and unemployed. Being unemployed during the off-season became a recurring theme in the mountains for my first few years in Vail. The town, a mere thirty years old when I moved there, was still working toward becoming a globally recognized, year-round resort destination. A ski mountain before ever being officially recognized as an actual city, Vail was still developing. I don't think anyone associated with Vail at this time in the late nineties could have predicted the global dominance that Vail Resorts and the Town of Vail were about to become.

While I was enjoying my recently acquired free time, back in Minnesota, my brother was quickly becoming a great financial success. Now married to Amy and the father of two boys, G.P.'s family was growing. They were in need of a bigger and better home. To help me financially survive Vail's off-season, my brother offered me a job helping him remodel and expand his house. While being paid cash under the table, the job was somewhat lucrative, but the days were long and often labor-intensive. G.P. was somewhat of a demanding boss and many of the days felt like I was being driven like a slave, but he was still family and it was money.

While I was back in Minnesota surrounded by my family, I missed the mountains. It became apparent that Vail was truly home to me, not Minnesota where I had spent the first twenty years of my life. Although I knew there was not a lot happening in Vail, I still wanted to be home again. So after about a month of helping out my brother, I drove the sixteen hours back to Vail. I wanted to be with my new family.

Toward the end of May, I was driving past a parking garage for Vail Mountain and noticed a group of guys around my age assembling wooden ramps. Out of curiosity, I stopped in to investigate, and to my delight, they were, in fact, erecting a temporary, seasonal skate park that would be free to the public.

The project was organized by the youth center located at the bottom of the parking garage and given a tiny budget. The group I saw consisted of skateboarders of all ages, ranging from as young as twelve to their early thirties, and they were mostly volunteers. I quickly jumped on the opportunity to help out. After all, I had experience building ramps since elementary school. I was excited to have the opportunity to get involved with the community, especially helping build something I'd loved my entire life. I hadn't been much of a skateboarder since around the time Sean and his family had moved to Michigan nearly ten years earlier. However, when I was living in Boulder, I was only a couple blocks from the legendary "Blue Park," nicknamed due to its color. So, I had previously rekindled my love affair with skateboards—at least a little bit.

In Colorado, particularly in Vail, I no longer felt like the out-cast I had been my entire time in Minnesota. Minnesota always felt like a boring daily grind to me, with no goal or dream to chase after. Graduate, get a job, get married, have kids, retire, and done. But that wasn't me. Even at a young age, I had always been looking for an adventure. Nearly everyone I met in Vail was on their own type of adventure; most of them had left all their friends and family many states away just like I had in pursuit of that adventure. I belonged in Vail.

As Vail was still developing, summers were still slow and finding work was rather difficult, especially as a young punk with no meaningful job training or education. Luckily for me, my new roommate, Kevin, who managed a local Domino's pizza joint, got me a job tossing pizzas. Domino's became my first experi-ence with the food industry. Although I now had a job, the major-ity of my free time was still spent at the skatepark.

To protect the ramps from the elements, the wood was topped with black sheet metal that baked in the hot Colorado sunshine. Not the ideal material. Not only was the sheet metal extremely slick, but when you fell, you would instantly sear your bare skin, causing painful burns. A near death sentence. Plus, the sun was blinding. The park felt one-dimensional, because you simply couldn't see heading toward the sun. Around six in the evening when the sun fell behind the mountain was when most of the skaters would come out. The evening was by far the most desirable time to skate, although it was extremely crowded.

The skate park was free to the public and unmonitored, how-ever for liability reasons, there was a helmet law that was strictly enforced during the early years of the park. The cops often drove by, and If you were caught skating the park without a helmet, it

was an instant fifty-dollar fine. Besides the fine, everyone understood just having the park was a privilege, and no one wanted
that taken away. However, many of us simply couldn't skate while
wearing a helmet, myself included. For me, it was a combination
of throwing off my balance and impeding my peripheral vision;
I hated skateboarding with a helmet on. There was a tall bank
ramp on the east side of the park near the entrance of the parking
garage, and anytime someone saw a cop driving in, they would
yell "five-oh," the slang term for a cop. When the warning went
off, everyone grabbed the nearest helmet, whether their own or
not, and put it on. If someone was skating at the time, another
skater would throw a helmet at them and they would pick it up, as
if they just fell. There was great camaraderie at the park.

During these evening sessions, I mainly avoided the crowded
street course and skated the small mini ramp in the corner of the
park. Growing up in a farm town with all my ramps, I lacked the
confidence to skate "street," and I was considerably more comfortable skating transition. During the many evening mini ramp
sessions, I became good friends with a girl named Celeste, who
worked for the youth center. Celeste, along with Diane, who was
the director of the youth center, were put in charge of organizing
Vail's first skateboarding contest. Although working as a pizza
cook for Domino's, Vail was still slow, and I wasn't given full-time
hours, so I volunteered to help Celeste organize the event.

The contest was intended to help raise funds to improve our
little skate park. Since it was a fundraiser, that basically trans-
lated to little to zero funds to work with. So, for the contest to
succeed, we were relying on donations. Along with scavenging
for prizes from the many shops around town, we were also in
search of volunteers of any kind. Using word-of-mouth and our

connections in the community, we got a couple of bands to play for free. As much as many of us hated the five-oh, the cops were still generous in donating hot dogs and burgers, along with their time, for the event.

I didn't feel like I was a well-rounded enough skateboarder to actually compete. I also lacked the confidence to compare my skating to the others, so I volunteered to be one of the three judges. Vail's first ever skate contest ended up being a great success, so we decided to make it an annual event. Not only did it raise money, but the contest also brought the community together. For the first time in my life, I was actually beginning to feel community support for skateboarders. Skaters were no longer just viewed as misfits; we were finally becoming accepted in society.

I arrived in Vail for only the second year of this amazing, little skate park's existence, and by the third year, we were able to afford to paint the dangerously slick and scorching hot sheet metal. I was a proud snowboard and skateboard bum. Being a bum in Vail was not something the locals looked down upon. We were all there because of our passion for the mountain.

# Chapter 6:

## Full Circle to Matterhorn

During these early years, I also threw a lot of house parties. Especially with the crazy backyard snowboard park fully equipped with a log ride over a fire pit. Our home, 1682 Matterhorn Circle, was becoming so legendary all you had to do was say "sixteen eighty-two" and it seemed everyone in town knew what you were talking about.

I was sitting on the front stoop one afternoon when I saw a black SUV with a U.S. Ski Team logo on the side creeping down the road. Driving the SUV was this gorgeous, hot blond, and she stopped right in front of our house. Perhaps if it wasn't a gorgeous blond driving I may not have approached the car, but I was a sucker for beautiful girls, so I had to ask her what was up, thinking maybe she needed directions. As it turned out, she was checking out our driveway for a small, independent film they were shooting. In the end of the comedic film, in an ironic scene, a car rolls down a driveway and runs over the main character. Our driveway was perfectly suited for the scene. After our short, five-minute conversation, I offered up our home for a full day of shooting.

A few days later, their team showed up at our house to film, setting up an entire buffet in our driveway. The team arrived early in the morning and prepared for a full day of shooting. I was a little shocked at the size of the production for what amounted to a short, two-minute scene in an independent film. For a young kid coming from a small farm community, our driveway felt like a big-time Hollywood production. Although our house was only in a quick scene at the end of the movie, it was still exciting. Sixteen Eighty-Two was now a movie star, too.

In the closing scene of the film, *Minimum Wage* directed by Jonathan Bricklin, the main character is smoking weed on a blue couch. My old blue couch. Out of my buddy's bong. And yes, the actor smoked real weed in the movie, even before it was legal.

A couple years later, we were evicted from that ghetto-fabulous house. I came home from the skate park one afternoon and saw a full-size letter taped to our door. As the story went, our landlord only wanted one check for rent, as we only had one lease between the four of us, so we had all been giving Kevin our rent money—assuming Kevin was writing our landlord a check and delivering it to him. I never sorted out the specific details, but Kevin must have had some financial issues of his own, as he was just pocketing the money.

But Kevin was a good guy at heart, and at some point during his financial struggles, he wanted to make things right. So late one night, while apparently drunk, Kevin decided to steal some money from the safe at Domino's. Maybe it was drugs or maybe it was the alcohol, but not only did Kevin leave his greasy handprint on the door, but he also completely forgot about the security cameras or even the fact that he was the only person other than the owners with a key. Either way, Kevin was quickly caught and sentenced to two years in a halfway house in Southern Colorado for his stupidity. So now Kevin was in prison, eating the vegetarian meals because he learned they were more substantial than the meals containing meat—while I was once again a homeless bum.

I had spent four years in Sixteen Eighty-Two. The household had been somewhat of a revolving door of roommates, as the place was small and quite run-down. My roommates were often looking for an upgrade. For me, however, I was rarely home, and four walls and a door was all I needed. Plus, I hated the hassle of trying to find a new place and packing up my belongings. After the eviction, everyone in the house went their separate ways, except C.J. and I. We decided to save some money and camp out for the summer to avoid paying rent. My camping only lasted about two weeks, though, because I conveniently started dating a chill, caring girl named Sarah.

I kept my tent set up all summer long, tucked away in the woods hidden from view, just in case, but I always stayed with Sarah. She had a job at a newly opened soup joint called Mizupa. The owner was an older chef/restaurateur who had retired three times and had owned more than a hundred restaurants over the years. It seemed like he just loved the industry and couldn't get away. Since I wasn't getting enough hours at Domino's, Sarah managed to get me a job with her at Mizupa. All the soups were made an hour away in Summit County, because we didn't have a full kitchen. However, all the bread was baked in-house and fresh everyday. Eventually I was moved from a soup slinger to a bread baker. Baking bread was a pretty good gig, as long as you could wake up early. I arrived around 5:30 in the morning and had the place all to myself, so I would blast punk rock and bake.

Mizupa was in a little strip mall in West Vail right next to a GNC. At GNC, a sweet, young girl would open up around seven in the morning. My blaring punk rock knocked GNC's bottles off the wall, so she frequently stopped by to ask me to turn it down. She was always nice about it and even laughed, so I considered it flirting. In my early twenties, I was still too irresponsible to be left unsupervised, but baking bread was simple. The bread had to proof for forty-five minutes every day, so I conveniently used this time to sneak out and have some early morning Bloody Marys at the nearby cafe. I was usually running on only about four hours of sleep a night, mainly because I loved the nightlife. I figured if I was late in the morning, I could take shortcuts, like cutting down that proof time or raising the temps and cutting down on that bake time. I took some shortcuts here and there, but the bread was turning out just fine.

Winter came along, and I was still "camping," but actually staying with Sarah every night. She proposed that I should start paying rent and move in with her. But the idea was quickly shot down by her roommate. The house would have been too crowded, and no one ever really wants to live with a couple. It didn't matter, though. I was always there, anyway, because I had nowhere else to go. It turned out Sarah was also too much of a free-spirited hippie with a caring heart, and she couldn't kick me out in the cold. So eventually, we all agreed I would start paying rent, officially making us roommates.

I don't think anyone could have possibly thought this crazy relationship could have lasted. I admit, I was in this relationship mostly out of convenience. I wasn't sure what Sarah was getting out of the relationship; we clearly weren't right for each other. Sometime during the middle of winter, we got in a fight. Sarah was all coked up and hanging out with her ex-boyfriend, and I kind of lost it when she didn't come home. She was with a group of friends, so the thought of her cheating on me wasn't really what bothered me. I looked her in the eyes, and they were extremely glossed over and dilated from the cocaine. I looked at her eyes that night and saw nothing there. She looked happy, but I could see all the way into her soul—quite literally, from how dilated her pupils were. At first, I felt upset about her not coming home, but now I knew I wanted nothing to do with her.

It was three or four in the morning, and I grabbed my belongings and stormed out the door. I carried everything I owned and walked three miles to where my old friends Hippie Abby, Reeeedtard, and another buddy, Slim Jim, were renting a three-bedroom condo. I slept on their couch that night. The next day, we made arrangements for me to move in.

By now, Abby and Reed were close family, so they instantly offered to help me. The condo had a little landing halfway up the stairs where I could fit a small, twin-sized mattress. I hung up a couple banners for privacy and started renting out this landing for three hundred bucks a month. It wasn't much, but it was my only option. Although Sarah and I eventually talked things over, we agreed we weren't right for each other.

I don't have a lot of memories from my time living on those stairs with Abby and Reed, but one of the memories I do have is of a girl I took home. She knew where I lived, but she didn't know what window was mine. She also didn't know our landlord lived directly below us. Around four in the morning, she was caught crawling through our landlord's window, trying to reach me. Luckily, he took it well—probably way better than I would if a random girl tried crawling through my window. She was just that: a random girl. Before the landlord incident, I took her home once. I couldn't remember her name then, and definitely couldn't remember it afterward.

Eventually, this household broke up, too. When we went our separate ways, I found my way back to Matterhorn, the 'hood where my story in Vail all started. By now, I knew quite a few people around town, and it seemed like someone was always looking for a roommate. I lived in a girl's attic for maybe a year; it was at least cheap rent. Then, I learned my friend, Emma (who was somewhat of a barfly like me), was living in a four-bedroom rental, part of a triplex located across the street from Sixteen Eighty-Two. Emma had an available bedroom for rent and offered it to me. I jumped on the opportunity to be back in that part of town. This was my favorite neighborhood, because it was a ski bum's paradise. Not only did the bus system give you quick access to the ski lifts, but you could also ski directly to your back door. Not to mention the frequent parties thrown all over the block.

Emma was from Lincolnshire, England, and had a thick accent. Living with her was Zeke, a Kiwi from New Zealand, and an eastern European girl named Petra. For the first time in my life, I was living in an international household—and I loved it. I was quickly taken in by my new housemates, and they felt like family. Petra was pretty quiet and kept to herself most of the time, while Zeke and Emma were huge dirt bikers. Every day, I heard the *braaaaap, braaapp* of their bikes in the air. I loved their passion for it. By this time my own passion for snowboarding was beginning to fade away. I still loved it, just not as much as I once had. The injuries were catching up with me, and snowboarding wasn't providing me with the rewarding challenge I was still getting from skateboarding.

Skateboarding was still my obsession. Many times, I stumbled through the front door as Emma and Zeke were watching some show about motorcycles, and my shoulder was out of the socket. I couldn't find anyone else to help me pop it back into place, so I would ask them to try. Usually, someone would just put their foot in my armpit and start pulling on my arm. It hurt like hell. Sometimes it worked; other times it didn't. One day, I was skating at an indoor park in Eagle about thirty minutes from Vail when I couldn't get my shoulder back in. I sat there for two hours with my shoulder out of the socket until the session was over and drove back to Vail with some other skateboarders. I had to give up and resort to making an appearance at the hospital.

During this time, I was also just beginning to live out my rock star fantasies, through my karaoke stardom. There was a dive bar in the Lionshead Village called the Sundance. Its slogan was "The Last Great Ski Bar." It really was a dive, so most locals referred to it as the Scumdance. I loved the place: cheap beer and the perfect bartenders to match. The Scumdance hosted a karaoke night once a week, and this was where I had my chance to put on a show. I loved pretending I was a rock star. Having no musical talent, I knew this was as close as I could get. Bon Jovi was usually a fan favorite, but I loved *Youth Gone Wild* by Skid Row and Alice Cooper's *Poison*. I felt like I was still a wild kid, the punk-skater hellraiser type—still a youth going wild.

Although I loved sticking to glam rock, I was also into pop punk, like Blink 182. My nickname Paul-Asian became my stage name. I liked to open my "show" with Blink 182's *What's My Age Again*? and replaced the lyrics with "Who's your Asian friend?" Vail had very few actual Asians, so it wasn't too offensive, and I'm Asian-American, so I figured it'd be fine. As a regular at kara-oke, I began to have a following; I actually had some groupies!

I was at karaoke one night with Emma, and she said she had something to show me in the ladies room. Someone had written "I LOVE PAUL-ASIAN" in huge print, taking up two square feet of the bathroom door. I was on my way to becoming a Vail legend.

I had been living with Emma for a while now, and my resume of jobs had started to grow as I rarely held on to a job for more than a few months. Jobs had either been only seasonal or not a good fit for me. Including the bakery. Whatever the case, I had worked jobs from landscaping to busing tables. Unable to hold onto a steady job, I was on the verge of poverty. I managed to keep a roof over my head, but I was basically living off free granola bars that were handed out at the weekly free concert series, along with the free food given away during Vail's Friday block parties at the top of Bridge Street in the center of Vail Village.

Then one day Emma looked at me, not one to hold anything back, and told me that I looked unhealthily skinny. I looked like a malnourished kid, and I needed a more substantial diet. I took her observation seriously. During this time, Emma saw me rummaging through the cabinets for what to make myself for dinner. It was through this rummaging that Emma noticed an unexpected potential. While I was simply "poor," I was forced to make delicious (or at least edible) meals out of nearly nothing. I was unaware of it at the time, but I was about to find my life-changing career.

On our famous blue couch with Reeeetard, Hippie Abby, and Drunk Rob

View from my judge's seat, one of Vail's skate comps

Boardslide at the Burton yurt

Front flip, our backyard sixteen eighty-two

Karaoke at the bar that made me famous,
Scumdance Saloon—The Last Great Ski
Bar

One of the last afternoon gatherings at Minnie's Deck

The last B. B. and B.

# PART 2

PART 2

# Chapter 7:

## You Will Be Next

Emma had been working as a server at an Italian restaurant called Vendetta's, located smack-dab in the center of Vail Village, in the heart of this world-class resort destination. Emma's recommendation landed me a job assembling salads in Vendetta's casual eatery. This job tossing salads opened the doors to an amazing life full of stories, adventures, and a bond of new, strong friendships with people who are no doubt my family 'til the day I die.

Vendetta's was mostly known for its popular pizza bar. Locals and tourists alike would grab a quick slice of pie and scurry off to the lift to make some quick turns, often returning hours later for drinks and to celebrate their great day on the mountain. Then, of course, in many cases, patrons would drink away their sorrows, pain, and injuries when days on the mountain were less than epic. Either way, there was always a reason to meet up at Vendetta's.

Vendetta's had been around since the early eighties and had developed quite the reputation for being the local watering hole. Many patrons drank excessively, as the staff often encouraged wild behavior, such as body shots. The raucous behavior resulted in Vendetta's earning the nickname "Regretta's," as the hungover patrons often regretted their behavior from the previous night. In addition to Vendetta's being popular for its prime location, Vendetta's was also the ski patrol's bar of choice.

Before the current owner of Vendetta's took over, the spot was owned by another legend of Vail named John Donovan. Donovan was one of the original locals who first moved to Vail in the sixties. Well into his eighties, Donovan could still be found giving mountain tours to tourists from around the world.

When Donovan opened the bar, it was nothing more than a tiny, little hole in the wall that he named The Copper Bar. The entire bar was covered with a brass metal lining that resembled copper, thus the name. It was at The Copper Bar where the tradition of a free "shift drink" for the ski patrollers emerged. It was the early eighties when the rumor surfaced that Vail Associates (later known as Vail Resorts) refused to give ski patrollers a raise. John Donovan , who was and still is a passionate skier, heard the news. Aware of the patrollers' hard work and dedication to assure a safe mountain, he began offering a free beer to every patroller after a day of work. The free drink went on to be simply known as "a raise." You could regularly see people walk up to the bar and ask for "a raise," and a bartender would pour a Bud draft on the house. When John Brennan, also an avid skier, took over the location to create Vendetta's, he continued the tradition. As a result, Vendetta's became a home for ski patrollers getting off of a hard day's work.

John Brennon was an old-school doorman in Vail, a large, well-built man. Although nearing his sixties, he still had an intimidating demeanor to him. With his massive forearms, John Brennon earned the nickname of "Popeye" from his rough and tough doorman days. Popeye's signature move was the one-hand choke slam against the wall, lifting the poor victim off his feet. He had an intimidating style of maintaining order. I recall a friend of one of my former roommates having a dispute over his bill. Popeye calmly offered to discuss the dispute "downstairs." Downstairs was where the formal dining room was located; it was open only for dinner hours and there were no windows and no witnesses. Popeye took the argumentative man off his feet, slamming him against the wall, letting him know he was never welcome in his restaurant, ever again.

I liked Popeye's aggressive, don't-give-a-fuck style. He was old-school. He reminded me of another era in history, the Wild West, a time when people governed themselves.

One of my favorite stories was a Fourth of July celebration in the middle of the day. Vendetta's had recently replaced the carpets, as the wear and tear of a busy restaurant requires new carpet every couple of years. It was on this warm July afternoon that Popeye was carrying some extra chairs up the stairs; it was a busy day. As Popeye turned the corner, he saw a belligerent drunk urinating on his freshly carpeted stairs. Popeye began by throwing the chairs at the culprit and proceeded to grab him by the neck, nearly squeezing the life out of him. With his massive forearms, Popeye slammed the man's face into his own fresh urine to rub his nose in the soiled carpet like a bad dog. If the smell of his own urine wasn't embarrassing enough, Popeye then threw the guy out into the middle of bustling Bridge Street with his pants still down around his ankles.

When later asked about the incident, Popeye simply responded, "He was pissing on my brand new carpet."

I couldn't help but agree; it seemed like a reasonable reaction to seeing a grown man acting like a young puppy.

Popeye was also known for his intimidating and aggressive

form of business ownership, often threatening to "rip your fuck-ing head off" if you got on his bad side. Many of us who had the pleasure of working for him simply called him "Pops." Pops as in a father figure, which was exactly how I thought of him. Just stay on his good side and you would have nothing to worry about. Not being a blood relative, Pops didn't treat me like I was a little kid. Pops treated me like the young adult I was. It was tough love and time to "be a man." Vendetta's was not the right work envi-ronment for everyone, but it was perfect for me. I wanted tough love. In my mind, Popeye was the perfect boss. He took good care of his staff, and as long as you were loyal to him, he would return the loyalty.

Having helped my brother remodel his house several years earlier, I knew what it felt like to be driven hard, but my brother was a blood relative. I knew he wanted the best for me. But working for Popeye, at first I had my doubts. What was I working for? Was I only being driven hard by his own interests? Did Pop-eye care about me at all? I was nothing more than a shy, punk kid assembling a few simple salads for him. With my brother, I was never worried about the life being choked out of me and be-ing thrown out the door. With Popeye, I wasn't so sure. He was an intimidating stranger who seemed bigger-than-life. To own a restaurant in the heart of a globally recognized resort destination was no small feat, and Popeye was pulling it off.

Running the main kitchen located in the basement was a friendly and caring Mexican man named Rafael, or Rafa for short. Popeye and Rafa were the yin and yang of all bosses, the good cop, bad cop of my superiors. Rafa had been with Pop-eye since nearly the beginning, having opened up the restaurant as a cook more than twenty years earlier. Popeye had recently thanked Rafa for his loyalty by making him part owner of the restaurant, as well. Possessing exactly what was required for a long and successful career in this industry, Rafa truly enjoyed making others happy. Before Rafa, a chef named Ray Jay had been the original opening head chef of Vendetta's. Ray Jay had recently retired from the kitchen and left the restaurant one year before I arrived at Vendetta's. However, I had always known of Ray Jay, as his signature slice, Ray Jay's Wave, was a favorite of mine.

Besides just knowing Ray Jay's name, I had known his son for several years, because we often skated the Lionshead park together. Ray Jay had married a few years earlier, and his wife consequently gave him somewhat of an ultimatum, convincing him to leave the industry, as she strongly objected to the life-style. I considered Vendetta's much more than just a restaurant. It was a new way of living. Vendetta's showed me what life was like to "live large." We lived like ballers. The drug use was rampant, and the parties were off the hook. All the veterans of the restaurant had adopted Popeye's larger-than-life attitude.

I was still a young, shy, somewhat sheltered kid from a small farm town in southern Minnesota. I was intimidated, yet knew I needed to fit in. Luckily for me, Emma was quite the opposite. She was a loud Brit, and as one of the veterans, she had a voice at Vendetta's. Emma was also a tough chick, so I doubt she was intimidated by anything. She helped me fit in, and I was ultimately referred to as "Emma's roommate."

I started off at a low hourly wage of $10 per hour. However, I was quickly given a dollar an hour raise, as they learned I was a relatively competent salad assembler. Rafa usually ran Vendetta's lunch service. Lunch was more casual than dinner service and was considered a better work schedule, as dinner often resulted in a late night's work. With Ray Jay's departure, dinner service responsibilities were taken over by Danny and Joe, who were in their mid- to late-twenties, only a couple years older than I was. But there was still a large gap in maturity. I was still new to the industry and a dedicated ski bum very used to avoiding responsibilities.

As the newbie or the "F.N.G." (fucking new guy), as we were often called in the industry, I was nervous about approaching the "hot line." I was hidden away in a separate pantry section. It may not have been so much as nerves, but at least I had enough respect for those guys to stay out of their way. At the time, Vendetta's had yet to adopt the industry standard of cooking one "family meal" for the entire staff to enjoy. Rather, the staff would ring in an employee meal to notify the kitchen they would like something to eat. As a back-of-house employee, we didn't ring in tickets; rather, we just made ourselves something to eat. I couldn't live off salads alone, so I often asked Danny to make me something. I wanted to stay out of the way of most cooks, and Danny seemed the most approachable. Joe was more intimidating: a classic, old-school-style chef not hesitant to yell at anyone for their ignorance.

Danny was from Argentina, and he passed through Miami on his way to Vail. Having grown up with Italian and Argentinian influences, Danny had a real passion for food and dining. After Vendetta's, Danny went on to go through a two-year culinary journey throughout Europe, including a six-month stage at Noma, the acclaimed Danish restaurant run by René Redzepi. This resulted in helping him open two acclaimed restaurants in Minneapolis with the James Beard award-winner Isaac Becker, and later opening two successful and popular restaurants of his own in Minneapolis called Martina and Colita. He went on to be nominated for a James Beard Award for the best chef in the Midwest—an award his mentor, Minneapolis chef and restaurateur Isaac Becker, had once received.

As Danny was traveling the world, building his resume along with a global network of industry connections, I stayed at Vendetta's. I wasn't ready to commit to becoming a chef. I was still a skateboarder first. Simply put, I had a lot more maturing to do. Vendetta's was helping me grow up, but I wasn't certain I wanted that. I enjoyed being a skater punk. It was all I'd known for as long as I could remember. Skateboarding was the one thing that gave me an identity, and I felt like becoming a mature adult would mean letting go of my greatest passion—and the sense of self I attached to it. Skateboarding was the main driving force that had gotten me to this stage in my life, and I wasn't ready to let it go. I was hesitant to accept my Vendetta's family into my life. This subconscious decision ultimately slowed down my development.

Eventually, once I got a little more comfortable in the Vendetta's kitchen, I had the courage to invade the space of the line to cook and make myself a meal. One afternoon, I made myself a little chicken curry dish with rice, a recipe my sister had taught me many years earlier.

Danny walked over and asked, "What's that?" I told him it was chicken curry, and delighted, he responded, "You will be next," meaning I would be next to move up the ranks.

Four simple words. It was the confidence boost that I needed. Danny must have known he was getting ready to move on, and I would soon be his successor. I had worked with Danny for less than a year, yet we created a strong friendship.

Danny was quite the ladies' man. Maybe it was his Argentinian accent or his natural charm. Whatever it was, women were all over him. After service, we often hit up the bars for a few drinks. I watched Danny as he flirted with all these hotties at the bar. Then the girls started coming over and flirting with me. I later learned, quite a few years later actually, that Danny had been telling the girls that I liked them. Needless to say, Danny made quite the wingman. Unfortunately for me, I was just too ignorant and inexperienced with women to truly embrace the situation. I was just a salad tosser in a new environment, so I still had relatively low self-confidence.

When Danny left Vendetta's, I was still an inexperienced line cook. It took me several more years before I finally was able to fill Danny's vacated position. Two other talented cooks, Scotty and Aaron, were brought back for their second stints at Vendetta's. Scotty was nicknamed "Pippen," after the legendary Bulls basketball player. Although they shared the same first name, that was about all they had in common. While Pippen the basketball player was a tall black guy around two hundred twenty pounds, Pippen the chef was tiny, about five-foot-five, white, and around one hundred thirty pounds soaking wet. Pippen did go on to open up a nice, little coffee shop, DJ's and Dahlias, in nearby Gypsum with his wife Anne. A disc jockey first, Pippen was a well-known local in Vail working mainly as guest DJ at many bars and clubs around town, but his weekly hip-hop show across the street from Vendetta's at the then-Daily Grind coffee shop was a huge hit. It was only fitting that he would open his own coffee shop, a modern version of the Daily Grind.

Then there was Aaron. I felt intimidated by him. I was still in my mid-twenties, so he was a bit older than I was. Although Aaron was a talented chef, my best memory of him had nothing to do with food. Aaron and Popeye were both large, intimidating figures who had worked together for a long time, at least long enough for me to consider them to be friends. One late night in Vendetta's, they challenged each other to an arm-wrestling match. The trash talking got personal and a fight broke out. I was nearby when the scuffle occurred, and I witnessed a pissed off Popeye tangled in the bar stools, bleeding from his forehead. As Aaron was leaving the bar, Popeye freed himself from the mess of barstools and chased Aaron down Bridge Street. I never knew if Popeye caught up with Aaron in the street or what happened next, but the dispute at least temporarily ended their friendship.

I only worked with Aaron for one winter. He was long over Vendetta's and ready to move on to something different. With both Danny and Aaron leaving Vendetta's, and then with Rafa primarily responsible for lunch service, it was up to Joe, Pippen, and me, a group of misfits, to ensure successful dinner services. At the time, we were all really just line cooks. However, Popeye put a lot of trust in us. We were a staff running on seniority, and I was still the F.N.G. All kitchens need some sort of structure, and Joe essentially had the most seniority, so he had his own days off. On Joe's days off, it was The Pippen and Paul Show. And it was quite the show. The two of us were often a shit show, far from executing a perfect service. We were too young to take anything we did seriously, and to succeed, you need to be dedicated. We just weren't.

When Pippen put in his notice to move to Vegas, my chance to move up the ranks was inevitable. I wasn't prepared, but in this industry, young kids are often thrown to the wolves. Sink or swim is the industry standard analogy. And I've been a part of many sinking ships. I remember Pippen giving me my first opportunity to produce my first dinner specials. I showed up one afternoon at my usual time of 4 p.m., and he looked at me, handed me a box of frozen steaks, and said, "Here you go. Have fun." Dinner service started at five, only one hour after I arrived. Pippen laughed, as he knew I was clearly fucked. I don't remember what I ran as a special, but I'm sure it was simple, because whatever I was going to do, all I knew was that I needed to get those damn frozen streaks aqua-thawing under some cold water. You can't properly cook a frozen steak.

Most of the specials the chefs created at Vendetta's were simple. Our time restraints were our main concern. With only an hour to create a dish—actually two dishes—before service, time was extremely limited. It was like being a competitor of the popular TV show *Iron Chef*, except we were preparing dishes for hundreds of paying guests. The key to succeed with such a daunting task was to keep things simple. Rafa was primarily responsible for the ordering and would often help us keep specials interesting by ordering various proteins to base our theme on. As a result, we often got to work with unique and exotic ingredients, such as venison or monkfish.

With the lack of communication, we rarely knew in advance what we had to use for specials. Although I know this was never intentional, it was just the reality of a busy restaurant with everyone living busy lives. The varying proteins were beneficial for us as cooks; although the components for our specials may have been simple, the star of the dish could be unique each night. The opportunity to work with new proteins nearly every night was a blessing. Very few chefs have the opportunity to work with as many different proteins as we had at Vendetta's. Veal, lamb, duck, and particularly when it came to fish. I have yet to find another restaurant that serves cobia, opah, or escolar, among many others. I began to consider fish to be more of my specialty.

I don't like to use the time restraints as an excuse, as I later learned every kitchen in the world has time restraints. Our specials were also simple as a result of a combination of the lack of knowledge, skill, and ambition. What I needed was to start with ambition and the other required tools would follow. Opening the communication doors was simple. It was just rarely done. I began asking Rafa what he had ordered for specials—such a simple task, but it had yet to be established as a standard practice at Vendetta's. Simply knowing what the focal point and foundation of the evening specials would be was paramount. Just a single day's notice, and the dinner chef could actually plan in advance.

I began taking a lot of pride in my dishes. For the first time in my life, I was given the freedom to express myself. During my time at Vendetta's, we never truly had a typical head chef—a chef with an ego who needed to put his stamp on every dish leaving the kitchen. Although I was without the title of head chef, I was beginning to feel like one, because my dishes were allowed to leave the kitchen without any further manipulation. I had total creative control of my creations. I was going with the flow of my career path, but I was well aware I was taking a much different route than the path most kids with the desire to become chefs take.

I had no culinary instructors telling me what to do or head chefs yelling at me to do it their way or leave. I was always too stubborn to learn that way. I was a hard-headed punk and hated following rules. Whether inside a kitchen, a classroom, or out on the streets, I was a rebel. My parents were still disappointed with me that I had dropped out of college. I was the first person in my family to not graduate. Knowing I was beginning to find my own career path, my parents even offered to send me to culinary school. I quickly shot down the offer. I knew I couldn't stand being told what to do. I needed to learn on my own. At Vendetta's, I found the perfect situation for me to succeed.

Although I was still inexperienced, I knew the basis of what would account for a good special. I needed to make the dish sound good, look good, and taste good. Knowing the three fundamentals for a good dish, I now needed to find my own personal inspirations. Since I was nothing more than a broke snowboard bum, eating out at fancy restaurants was not an option for me. Low ambition and poverty were both contributors to my slow development in the field of cooking. Although I was unable to afford dining out, most restaurants posted their menus outside, and going around town reading menus was free. I'm not sure how much reading menus at the time really helped, because my food knowledge was limited, but it was an attempt at free education.

Pippen recommended I buy a copy of *The Food Lover's Companion* by Sharon Tyler Herbst, a dictionary of culinary terms. Although a paperback and small in size, this book contained a ton of useful information, therefore it never left my locker at work. I was learning culinary terms and ingredients as I went along, and so much information became impossible to retain. However, whatever I needed to know at any particular time, I had the information at my fingertips. Before smartphones, I had nothing but this little book, which became a lifesaver.

For a long time, *Food Lover's Companion* was the only book I owned. It was all I felt I needed. Then David Walford, a local chef, released his first cookbook, *Wood Fire and Champagne Powder: Colorado Cuisine, Elevated.* Steamboat Ski Resort had trademarked the term "Champagne Powder," and they took Walford to court. Walford and his lawyer had no chance against Steamboat's powerful team of legal professionals. As a result, he was not allowed to sell his book. I had quite a few friends working at his restaurant, Splendido, including my good skating buddy, Quintin. Although not legally allowed to sell his book, giving the book away for free was a perfectly viable option. So I acquired a free copy, and *Wood Fire and Champagne Powder* became my first cookbook.

Although I was now beginning to develop a career, my run-ins with the law continued. As Vail was undergoing a major transformation into the twenty-first century, old hotels were being torn down and being replaced with new luxury resorts, such as the Four Seasons and the Arrabelle. As the old hotels were being demolished, their swimming pools were being drained. Scouring for empty swimming pools to skate became my new obsession.

One night, several of my friends and I were skating an empty pool directly across the street from the fire department. We had a case of beer with us and were settled in, skating the pool for two hours, when the police pulled up, blocking our only exit. We decided to take off running into the abandoned hotel. Inside the building, we split up, increasing the odds for at least some of us to escape. Silly Billy, who was skating the pool with us, found a way out through an emergency exit. Having to use our cell phones for light, I was trapped in what appeared like a small garage with my buddy Jay. While stuck in the dark, Silly Billy sent me a text on how to escape. But as I opened the emergency door, the police were waiting. We took off running. We ran in the direction of the fire department, and we were cornered. Once again, I was headed to spend the night in the police station.

# Chapter 8:

## Once-in-a-Lifetime Adventures

With my new job, I had finally found financial stability, so I was able to save up some money. Recently, my friend Jen had moved to Hawaii for school. Having grown up in frozen, landlocked Minnesota, I'd always had a fascination with tropical islands, so I decided to plan a two-week vacation.

My vacation to Hawaii was not only my first "real" vacation as an adult, but it was also my first trip for culinary inspiration. I flew to Hawaii and ate absolutely nothing but local cuisine. I tried poke and musubi for the first time. I ate fish, as well as spam. I was hooked on Hawaii's version of sushi. I literally ate it every day. I found an infatuation with kalua pig, too—from wrapped in banana leaves to slowly roasted and buried in a hole. Smokey, moist, and unbelievably tender, kalua pig on a true Hawaiian pizza was amazing. With the "plate lunches," affordable and served virtually everywhere, I was in heaven. To me, Laulau, which translates to leaf leaf, symbolized the true essence of Hawaiian food. Pork belly and fish wrapped in taro leaves and steamed for hours until the leaves were so tender they became mush—the aroma of the dish just screamed the tropics.

I not only fell in love with the food, I also fell in love with the island vibe. I took a trip up to the legendary North Shore and

Waimea Bay. There, I felt the most nostalgic feeling of my life. Seeing all the shrines of the local people who had passed away over the years, I could feel the humbling respect being given to the ocean. The entire island had a unique aura about it. This was the most famous and universally recognized as the best surfing in the world. I learned they measured the waves differently; they start the measurement at six feet, or head high. So a three-foot break really means nine-foot waves. They are massive in Hawaii. I'd always been terrified of the ocean, whether it was from sharks (watching Jaws freaked me out) or simply the power of the ocean. But conquering fears is probably my greatest joy in life. Being a skateboarder, I felt my life would be incomplete if I didn't at least attempt to surf.

So Jen took me to a semi-private beach that only the locals knew of. I decided to try out her longboard, considering it should be much easier to learn on. As I was paddling out, I suddenly dislocated my shoulder and realized my arm couldn't move in the way required to paddle. I screamed in extreme agony, eventually popping my shoulder back in place while still out on the water. As I returned to shore, the locals said they thought I just had the cramps. I then remembered Bethany Hamilton, a pro surfer who had her arm bitten off by a shark just the year before. Bethany was able to still surf using only one arm to paddle, so I knew it was possible. I paddled out to the surf using only one arm. After a few failed attempts, I realized that I didn't know the fundamentals to catch a wave. My timing wasn't right. Although I was never able to surf, island life was still paradise.

Jen's apartment was located high up in the hills. While Jen was at class, I often skated down the long two- to three-mile hill all the way to Waikiki. Swerving through traffic, it felt like how I had always imagined skateboarding through the streets of San Francisco would be. Once I arrived at the boulevard running along the touristy area of Waikiki, I was once again harassed by the police. Honolulu had an ordinance against skateboarding in Waikiki, and I wasn't aware of this. The police thought I looked like a local and assumed I should know better. After checking my Colorado I.D., they let me off with a warning.

This was not the only time people thought I was a local on the island. As I drove around in Jen's sticker-covered station wagon, I would pull up to the beach and locals would instantly start up a conversation, talking about the surf. To their surprise, I had to cut the conversation short, as I explained to them that I wasn't from the island, and I had no idea how to surf. Hawaiians usually hate "howlies," or foreigners, but I looked the part and was fitting in.

Returning to Vail, Vendetta's was becoming an immense success, as the restaurant was reaching its twenty-five-year anniversary. In celebration, Popeye planned an extensive facelift for our outdated dining room. The dining room looked like a strip club from the eighties, with more than just copper accents, but a full copper roll top ceiling. Popeye later professed that had Vail zoning codes allowed it, he would have opened the bar as a strip club. In reality, the facelift needed to occur much sooner. The decor was damn right appalling.

A much more modern look had been in the works for quite some time, and the construction began. Most of the copper was replaced with beautiful stained wood. Gorgeous bricks added nice contrast, the shelf above the bar was removed, making the room feel less claustrophobic, and a gorgeous wine rack was included next to the stairs. In addition to the modern upgrades to the dining area, building and fire codes required that our hand-icap-accessible restroom be functional. We had been using the restroom as backup liquor storage, and apparently that was un-acceptable. With the upgrades, this was the beginning of a new era for Vendetta's.

To celebrate our anniversary and the recent remodel, Popeye decided to throw a massive party. The party was an invite-only, ticket-required event with an open bar and free food. I heard rumors that Popeye had given out nearly six hundred tickets, despite the fire code limit of less than two hundred. Whether the rumor was true or not, the party was packed to the walls. This would be my first time experiencing a true Vendetta's bash, and I quickly learned Popeye knew how to throw a great party. You might think a pizza party with free beer would suffice, but not for Popeye. He preferred to celebrate with an unlimited open bar and bottles of wine and champagne being passed around the room. As for the food, we served calamari, shrimp, lamb, and mini osso bucos, which I hadn't even known existed until this party. As a kitchen employee, we were responsible for not only preparing the food, but the service, as well. Although I missed out on most of the fun, serving the food banquet-style, I was at least able to mingle with the guests and enjoy a few adult bev-erages in the process. This was one of the few occasions where drinking on the job was not only allowed, but encouraged.

I would have gladly kept living with Emma, however our liv-ing arrangement was about to end. After I returned home from vacation in Hawaii, rumors had surfaced that I was planning on moving to the islands. The idea had definitely crossed my mind, especially when the ticketing agent told me my flight back to the mainland was delayed five hours. Jen was also looking for a new place to live and suggested the two of us moved in together. I took the two circumstances as a sign, and I was close to making Hawaii home. But in the end, it just wasn't ready to happen quite yet. So with my future in question, Emma decided to find a new home without me, and I was once again homeless. Rather than find my own place, I decided to buy a car off my friend's wife and make the car my new home. I had a temporary solution, because surviving a winter in Vail living out of your car is unfeasible.

The decision was to save money. Although I was working five days a week at the restaurant, I could still use the extra money. Joe had been working for Ray Jay, Vendetta's original chef. He was painting, and they needed extra help. The timing could not have been any better for me. Ray Jay picked up a large job painting the exterior of an apartment complex. With the apartment complex as a construction site, I was able to park my car there all summer long. As a bonus, I could wake up in my car and conveniently already be at work, while doubling up on the money I was capable of saving. It was the perfect situation. As I saw it, without a home, I might as well just work. Working two full-time jobs while not having to pay rent or even have time to spend my money resulted in the most money I had ever been able to save.

Painting wasn't the only second job I had while working at Vendetta's. I also took up photography—which led me to some unbelievable snowboarding adventures. I was friends with a semi-pro snowboarder named Danny G, who I called Small Print Danny G and Danny Two Page. Whenever Drop gloves, one of his main sponsors, included his name in their ads, it was written in small print underneath other bigger-name team riders. In addition, the company only bothered to include his name when taking out a two-page ad. I liked to tease him that the company wouldn't even waste the ink unless they had an extra page to fill. Then one day, local Emage Magazine did a nine-page write-up on him. Naturally, he threw that in my face: "Ha! I'm Danny nine-page now."

The previous photographers Danny had worked with were charging too much, so as a friend, I volunteered my time and film, as I was still learning to shoot photos with my brand new technical Canon SLR. We traveled to backcountry locations and contests to shoot photos, then traveled to Vegas for the Snowsports Industries America trade show to kiss his sponsors' asses. Danny was more passionate about snowboarding than anyone I have ever met.

On one particular trip to Vegas for the trade show, they decided to hold a rail jam in the parking lot of the Hard Rock Hotel and Casino. After hauling in truckloads of snow, they built a ramp for a drop-in to hit the rails. The organizers of the event decided to set up two hot tubs at the top, inviting many strippers and bikini-laden beauties to frolic in the bubbly water. While competitors were attempting to slide the rails, others gathered at the top to party with the naked and near-naked ladies. Enjoying cheap beer and bottles of champagne, few of us even realized a contest was going on. They were failed dreams of making any substantial amount of money, but the experience was worth every roll of film I used.

My favorite trip was out to Lake Tahoe for a Boarding for Breast Cancer contest, a nonprofit founded in 1996. With iconic snowboarders and eighties legends Tina Basich and Shannon Dunn as spokeswomen, I was more than excited for this trip. I had grown up with a large poster of Tina Basich, the "godmother of snowboarding," on my wall. I'd had a crush on her since I was in middle school.

Then, earlier in the year I had the opportunity to meet her during the World Snowboarding Championships in Vail. I was far from starstruck when I met her. Unfortunately, the truth is I was extremely drunk after drinking four liters of Dunkel at a nearby German joint. When I met Tina, she was sweet, down-to-earth, and with her new, modern look, she was even more beautiful in person than how I remembered her on my wall. She had recently been featured in Maxim magazine, and was newly single after breaking up with Dave Grohl from the Foo Fighters.

Tina asked me out on a ride date for the next morning. She actually asked me out! But I didn't make it. I was too hungover and slept in. I stood her up—one of the biggest regrets of my life. When I saw her again later that weekend, after standing her up, she raised her hands and gave me a "What the fuck?" look. She probably had never been stood up before, and I never thought I would stand up the girl of my dreams.

Knowing Tina was a spokeswoman for Boarding for Breast Cancer, I was hoping to see her again in Tahoe. No such luck. I never saw her again.

Now with money in savings, I was given the opportunity to take time off and travel to the Philippines for the first time since my childhood. The journey was a long trip to the other side of the planet; twenty-five hours later, I arrived at the capital city of Manila. Once there, I met up with my parents and my sister, along with her new fiancé, Chris, and his brother, Evan. The three of them had just taken a brief exploration detour through Japan before meeting us on the island of Luzon. Once in Manila, for a mere $9 a day, we hired our own personal driver while in the city.

As we checked into nice hotels or went out for fancy dinners, our driver would just stay in his van. Everywhere we went, our driver waited for us. As Americans, we felt a little empathy for him and invited him to join us for dinner. Perhaps it was a cultural thing, possibly as a sign of respect or maybe professionalism, but our offers of kindness were always rejected.

I was the last of our family to arrive, so while the others were rested, I had gotten zero sleep and was possibly suffering from jet lag. I don't know how to relax, and I'm too anxious to be able to sleep on planes, even on the longest of flights. However, the lack of sleep wasn't going to stop me from hitting the town upon my arrival. My sister was never the type to enjoy the late-night shenanigans, but fortunately for me, her fiancé and his brother were down for a little adventure. Around midnight, the three of us left our posh hotel in downtown Manila and hit the streets. Our first stop was a nearby market so we could buy ourselves some Red Horse Beer, the only beer they seemed to carry in the entire city.

Walking around late at night, we asked the locals where we could go for a good time. All we were looking for was a bar. Then we ran into a promoter working the streets. He didn't seem to speak any English and directed us into what looked like the lobby of a hotel. The front desk then directed us to an elevator that took us up a floor. Upon the opening of the doors, we were greeted with a large, mostly empty room. We had not been directed to a bar, but rather thirty to forty girls sitting in the room. It appeared to be an Asian whore house. Initially we froze; all of us were speechless. Once we gathered our composure, none of saying a word, we silently freaked out and turned around. It was a shocking experience. None of us were looking for that kind of a good time. We finally found a bar nearby, which just happened to be a karaoke bar. I was already a karaoke rock star in Vail, so I figured it was a good time to finally take my show international.

All the employees at the bar were gorgeous young girls, and as it turned out, Filipino girls absolutely loved American boys. Picking up girls at this karaoke bar was about as effortless as it would ever get. We managed to attract three girls to join us for the entire evening; one of the girls was even the manager of the bar. After the karaoke bar closed, the girls took us to an all-night bar, where we danced and drank until the sun came up.

It was now around nine in the morning, and the girls joined us for the walk back to the hotel. After arriving at the hotel, Chris told the girls good night and that it was time to leave. It was an obvious decision for him, as he would soon be marrying my sister, but for me and Evan, it wasn't the way we would have preferred the night to end. However, we exchanged email addresses and thanked the girls for a good night.

By this point, I had already been awake for two days, and I was ready to pass out. Back in the room, we got a couple hours of shut-eye—literally only two or three hours. Manila was not our final destination. We had another plane to catch to the beautiful, touristy island of Boracay. The brief sleep was just long enough for me to wake up with what was probably the worst hangover of my life—a torturous experience when we boarded our tiny prop-driven plane. The plane was by far the sketchiest aircraft I have ever seen. We joked about the plane being propelled by what seemed like a lawn mower engine. With the plane flying at under 10,000 feet, we kept the windows open, so the fresh air was quite nice, but the noise from the engine combined with my hangover made me want to die. I was relieved that the flight was a short one. With my head absolutely throbbing, I couldn't wait to get off that plane.

We arrived at our beachside hotel, one of the nicest on the island, and we were greeted by a large sign welcoming the Alvero family. I loved the personal touch. For only $100 a night, it felt like we were being given the royal treatment. I had my own personal room, which was perfect for me, particularly because I often preferred to wander off and do my own thing. My own thing would usually consist of me just relaxing on the beach during the day and having a nice dinner at night, followed by a few drinks for a night cap. I have always hated doing the "tourist thing" and being on a schedule. Not my kind of vacation.

The beach at Boracay was absolutely beautiful, a picture-perfect place with unbelievably soft white sand and crystal clear blue water. It was a once-in-a-lifetime kind of vacation, so I couldn't help but at least do a few other once-in-a-lifetime adventures. We went parasailing, three hundred feet above the South China Sea, enjoying the amazing views. After parasailing, we went island-hopping with locals in a tiny catamaran and enjoyed a picnic-style lunch, eating freshly caught fish at local restaurants, which were nothing more than wooden shacks with grills and picnic tables.

One evening, I decided to treat myself to an amazing meal. My typical vacation budget generally only allowed for one nice meal per trip. Although I would often have many decent meals, only one could be special. After walking around the island, particularly up and down the beach, I stumbled across all these two-top tables spread out around the beach. It was late in the evening, and the only lighting was tiki torches and small candles, which were placed on each individual table, a romantic setting. The restaurant appeared as though I could actually enjoy a nice meal, with the calming view of the tables spread a good distance apart, rather than the sight of a bustling restaurant with the cling of silverware, glasses banging together, and plates being dropped on tables with zero finesse.

As I approached the entrance where a host would greet me, I witnessed one of the most beautiful things my eyes would ever see: a glass ice case featuring the freshest seafood available anywhere. How most restaurants I was accustomed to displayed their menu at the entrance, this restaurant displayed its fresh seafood. The restaurant had no menu. I was instructed to pick out my protein of choice and was escorted to my table. Although the beautiful Japanese spiny lobsters looked unique and intrigued me, I was yet to become a true culinary connoisseur. Rather, I opted for a gorgeous bright pink fish that the locals then called Lapu-Lapu. Although not quite as adventurous as the spiky crustacean, the bright fish with an exotic name seemed more like the type of fish you would keep as a pet in an aquarium than eat for dinner. The Lapu-Lapu was adventurous enough for me.

Once seated, a few minutes passed and a perfectly cooked Lapu-Lapu arrived at my table. Gently cooked over an open fire, the skin was perfectly crisp with a slight char and a very light smokey flavor. Served on a bed of tender rice with local calamansi limes, the dish was the simplest presentation of any dish I have ever received at a restaurant. This simple preparation of fish was the best I had ever eaten. The Lapu-Lapu had amazing sweetness and was succulently moist, a perfect flake that wasn't stringy. The texture had an amazing mouth feel. This dish taught me that beauty in food can be achieved through simplicity, rather than constantly relying on complexity to impress your diners.

Besides the perfect dish, there was also the perfect ambiance, with the flickering candlelight and the gorgeous silhouette of the calm sea and soft white sand under my feet. It was the perfect dining experience.

Just like in Manila, meeting local girls in Boracay was easy. I went out for a few drinks with Evan one night, and we found ourselves accompanied by many local girls. Perhaps Evan found a girl he especially hit it off with or possibly he just loved the island, but he chose to stay a few extra days. I considered spending more time on the island with him, and Evan tried his best to talk me into it, but I had traveled to the other side of the world for my family and wanted to explore more.

Returning to Manila, we then made the two-hour drive north to my dad's hometown of San Pablo. Although the drive was two hours long, the distance was more like forty-five miles with the congestion and traffic that had just gotten so bad over the years. My parents still own the house in San Pablo, the same house my dad grew up in and helped build in the sixties. By American standards, the house would be a typical middle-class home, but in the Philippines, this was a mansion.

In San Pablo, surrounded by nothing but mud shacks, stood our large, three-floor, five-bedroom home. With its two kitchens, a standard for upper-class Filipino families, one kitchen was open-air with mud floors, used to break down whole animals, while inside, there was a normal tiled kitchen with modern equipment that you would see in the states. In the states, we are often sheltered from real cooking: the nose-to-tail movement of using whole animals. In many other countries, if you are going to kill an animal, you are going to use the whole thing. I fully believe in this philosophy. Breaking down a whole animal is an important skill to learn, and it's a standard practice for most Filipino families.

As I continued to explore my dad's hometown, I was taking in as much of the Filipino culture as possible. Although I am against animal cruelty, as part of my cultural trip, it was a must to experience a live cock fight: roosters let loose in an inclosed arena and battling it out. It was a relief to learn that, although many people in the Western world believe the fight is to the death, many roosters survive to fight another day.

We also explored local cuisine: food carts that lined the streets and Asian markets, which are just markets when you are in Asia. The only American food we could find was McDonald's. I had always grown up eating Filipino food. My mom was an amazing cook, and we often had Kare-kare, Dinuguan, and, of course, the Filipino national dish of Adobo. There was still one certain Filipino delicacy I had yet to discover: Balut, a common street food that looks like nothing more than a large boiled egg at first glance. As I cracked open the shell, I saw the most un-appealing snack I could have ever imagined. Because Balut is a cooked duck embryo. If you have a strong stomach, picture a tiny (as though malnourished) only partially developed little bird. In the enclosed shell, the bird appears curled in the fetal position.

At first, my reaction was simple: Why? Why the hell would they wait until the bird is just barely starting to develop to cook it? My next thought was, Well, I've gone this far, so what the hell; may as well put it in my mouth. Once the little bird was in my mouth, had my palate not been sensitive to textures, I might have thought nothing of it; this was just a hard-boiled egg, right? Balut does taste like a hard-boiled egg. Only, you need to get over the fact that you can feel tiny bones cracking in your mouth, and when you are finished, you need to pull the feathers out of your teeth. After my experience with Balut, I would definitely say it is a must-try when you are in the Philippines. And now that I have, I never have to try another one as long as I live.

I also got to see our coconut plantation, with cows roaming freely, sipping on water from a stream. My parents had given up their dual citizenship, limiting the amount of land we could own, so only a small portion of the plantain remained ours. The plantation was mostly unkempt, which was actually a welcoming sight, a natural look and not commercialized. I loved that aspect of it.

We visited my Grand Uncle, who had a hobby of growing his own Bonsai trees. I remembered Bonsai trees from the Karate Kid movies and had always thought of them as an exotic plant from a far-away land. To see the trees in person was a reminder of how far away from home I was. The trees seemed to be the epitome of a mysterious foreign country.

Later that evening, we were treated to dinner at my dad's uncle's resort in the countryside. We arrived at the restaurant, and the entrance was a large garden, with tall foliage and vines towering over our heads. It was absolutely enchanting. The restaurant had an amazing ambiance with that unforgettable garden entrance, transforming an otherwise casual restaurant into magic. We were seated at a large table near the kitchen and given no menus. Food was just delivered to our table. Everything was served family-style, in large casserole-style dishes and on platters. This was another perfect meal, stressing the importance and beauty of eating as a family.

During the long flight home, I had plenty of time to let sink in what I had just witnessed. As I sat in the airplane, unable to sleep, I realized my life dream: creating a restaurant inspired by the meal on the beach in Boracay became my goal. I wanted to own my own magical dining experience: a restaurant featuring simple food. Relaxed and unpretentious. I knew cooking at a high level is not sustainable for the long term, so this became my retirement plan.

*When* I would be prepared to make my dream a reality became my only uncertainty. Although I now had a dream in my sights, I knew I was not quite ready. Traveling became the single most important thing I could do to develop as a chef.

# Chapter 9:

## Rock Star Lifestyle

Around the time Tony Hawk began his "secret skate-park tour," we decided to make our own skating vacation tradition. A couple years earlier, two of my friends took a similar tour: traveling across several states, hitting up the best skate parks they could find along the way. These were the same parks that Tony Hawk and his crew documented in his video series. I missed their first couple of trips, but I wasn't going to miss another. With the restaurant closing for its annual Lake Powell trip, I had the free time to cram in a rented passenger van with six other dudes and hit the road.

We were dirty rock stars on the road. On my first trip, we hit nineteen skate parks in twelve days across six states. We skated a monstrosity in Hailey, Idaho, with its massive, fourteen-foot transitions and its full pipe. It was like nothing I had ever seen before. The park was nearly un-skateable because of its sheer size. We also skated the iconic park, Burnside, in Portland, Oregon, which is credited for starting it all: the movement, with the bowls and concrete park, that transformed skateboarding forever.

We were sweaty, skating eight hours a day in blazing heat while driving close to five thousand miles. We were dirty. We were rolling even dirtier with the amount of booze and weed we were consuming. To say we were a little dirty was an understatement. Eventually, we met friends who let us at least shower at their homes or knew a few spots with camp showers. Evil Dave even came up with the idea to just buy new socks at Walmart and just throw them away after a single use. Socks were cheap, and there's nothing better than the feeling of fresh socks.

We made it all the way to Orcas Island in the San Juans, just off the coast of Washington state. Just as we were getting off the ferry, we picked up a cute, seventeen-year-old hitchhiker. As we opened the door of our van, first a two-foot-tall stack of skateboards fell over, followed by a pile of empty PBR beer cans, which the skateboards were holding in. After the massive stack of cans hit the street, a huge wave of weed smoke followed. I couldn't help but wonder what that poor girl was thinking. What was her first impression? At least we didn't scare her away. She got in our van full of smelly skateboarders, all of which were in our thirties. Maybe she had some of her own problems. I'm not sure, but she wanted to show us some natural hot springs on the island. We never took her up on the offer, as it seemed a bit risky to us. She was only seventeen! We had been on the road for nearly a week now, were in bad need of a shower, and the hot springs sounded amazing. But we opted not to let a teenager show us a good time. Instead, we searched for the hot springs on our own. We never found them.

Still, on our way up to our camp spot, we passed some coin-operated camp showers. We were finally saved from our own stench. Our campsite was a short hike from the road, which was when we realized we may have brought too much crap. Particularly Robby, who packed as though he was going to Alaska for a month. Why the hell did he need a damn parka on a skate trip? The rest of us felt the need to each have his own personal thirty pack of beer, as if we were spending two weeks rather than two days on the island. Carrying all the beer up the trail was a chore. So, of course, we now felt obligated to drink all the beer at the campsite so we wouldn't have to carry it back down.

Orcas Island skatepark was a special place. The park was a collaboration of effort and funding from numerous sources. Teams from Grindline and Dreamland skateparks, normally in competition with each other, joined forces. Funding came from major corporations, such as Oakley. However, there was no evidence of those responsible. On the outside of the park was a simple bronze plaque with a quote: "There is no limit to the amount of good you can do if you don't care who gets the credit," words I have gone on to live by.

We ended up staying on the island for five days, as we brought too much beer to leave, not to mention that Orcas was an amazing place. Although we were in the northwest, it still felt like the "island life" with a laid-back vibe. We skated the park every day we were on the island. On the short drive up from the skate park, there was a small stand outside a gas station selling fresh oysters. The island was surrounded by oyster farms. In my opinion, the best oysters in the country come from the cold waters of Washington. They are sweeter and less briny than their East Coast cousins. However, before Orcas Island, I knew nearly nothing about oysters. I was introduced to oysters on this trip.

On the first night after returning from the skate park, we noticed a group of young kids had set up camp within a few feet of ours. The kids were only around ten years old, so we assumed there would be adult supervision. We were the epitome of true "skate punk"—so we were a little nervous about our late-night shenanigans. After all, we had more than two hundred beers and handles of hard liquor between the seven of us. Shit had the potential of getting pretty crazy.

We managed to keep it together, and the kids just so happened to be pretty damn good crabbers. Yes, these ten-year-old kids knew how to catch crabs! They helped us pull fresh, live, rock crabs out of the Puget Sound, and crabs were the perfect main course to go with our oysters. Camping on the island, we had some of the best food of the trip. The crabs were delicious, but the oysters were inspiring. Oysters are often eaten raw; however, I quickly discovered the magic of gentle smoking. We placed the oysters on the rocks that formed our fire pit and let them smoke. Imparting the smoke was only one benefit. The fire was perfect for firming up the oysters, providing the perfect texture. Store-bought, smoked oysters are way overpowering and overcooked, but these were perfect. The oysters were quite frankly addictive, and we couldn't make a trip past that gas station without buying a few dozen each time.

My good friend, Quintin, was the chef of the trip, as I was just beginning to discover my passion for food. Quintin was working as sous chef at David Walford's ultra-contemporary, fine-dining establishment, Splendido, at the Chateau in Beaver Creek, and Quintin undoubtedly knew food. Like my old friend Danny, Quintin had traveled the country working at restaurants in California and Oregon, expanding his culinary knowledge and skills, before settling down at Splendido. Judging by Quintin's skating, I could tell he was not only talented, but creative as well. It was only fitting that Quintin would go on to be an amazing chef in his own right.

A few years after leaving Splendido, Quintin relocated to open his own restaurant in Pennsylvania, offering a single, seasonal tasting menu each night. Quintin, along with his wife, Liz, aptly named their restaurant Revival Kitchen, as they set out on a mission to revive the dining scene of central Pennsylvania by collaborating with local, primarily Amish farmers. Revival Kitchen is a true farm-to-table restaurant supporting the local community.

Halfway through our trip, we reached Portland, and that was when we really let loose. After minimal interaction with the opposite sex for a whole week, we were ready to let some testosterone fly. Portland was known for its strip clubs, and four strip clubs in one night was our mission. Including the famous Mary's Strip Club, a tiny dive where the girls play their own music through the jukebox. The back of the club was full of homeless people, and I didn't see a single sign of security as we entered. It appeared as if no one but beautiful girls worked there. The seven of us took the stage seats, literally occupying the whole row. We showed up and made it rain. The girls loved us and were intrigued. *"Who are these guys?"* We felt like true rock stars on the road.

I made it on two of those skate trips, and each was a unique adventure, providing legendary stories of what you would expect when you put seven testosterone-filled guys in a van for two weeks straight. The second trip, we followed a similar route, except with more back roads and hot springs. It was our own story of the life of skaters on the road, a life well- documented during *Thrasher Magazine's* King of the Road contest and later showcased on Vice. Although our experience was not a "contest," we recreated our own King of the Road adventure. We were constantly filming, in an attempt to put together our own skate video. Pulling into gas stations, the sight of a video camera would provoke girls to flash us their boobs, trying to make it in our video. Fueled by excessive drinking and weed smoking, we were raising hell on the road.

However, my life as a skateboarder was beginning to fade, as I was breaking down, not only physically, but mentally as well. The summer prior, I had smacked my head hard on the concrete in the Edwards skate park. The day of the accident, it was rather early in the morning. I remember being quite hungover, and my memory of the fall is a blur. I was knocked unconscious. I woke up in a puddle of blood with a gash in my head. It was wrapped in gauze, and the paramedics were kneeled down next to me asking questions.

"What's your name?"

"Do you know where you are?"

What scared me the most was that I remember thinking, *Shit. I don't know what my name is.* I responded with a somewhat dick attitude and said, "Fuck, it doesn't matter what my name is."

Although I didn't know my name, I knew I didn't have insurance and couldn't afford a trip to the hospital. I was worried they would make me go, so I stood up and skated away.

It was a concussion. It scared me, but I thought I was fine. I had to fill out some paperwork and my friend, Celeste, signed off for me. Therefore being responsible for my safety, Celeste made me stay on her couch until I was better. I'd had many concussions over the years, but this incident made me question my risk-versus-reward balance.

I wasn't quite ready to slow down, though. A few months later, on one of our skate trips, I smacked my head at the Bainbridge Island Skatepark, just a few Islands down from Orcas. I was simply warming up in the small part of the bowl, preparing to attempt a trick in the larger section, as we were filming. Although not nearly as serious as my previous injury in Edwards, the fall affected me mentally. My confidence was down. I no longer felt invincible.

My second year on the road would be our last, and a much different skate trip than the year before. A different crew and poor weather were the primary culprits for a more relaxed and less intense skating experience. The Pacific Northwest was notorious for endless weeks of rain, but we had been lucky the previous year with perfect weather. Particularly on Orcas, however, this year was nonstop downpours. Unmotivated to skate because of the rain and not willing to spend our days confined to our tents, we hit up the bars on the island. We stumbled across a karaoke bar, and I attempted to put on a show in the way a rock star wannabe would do it. By the time the bar closed, we were all heavily intoxicated. As we stumbled into our van, it was clear we were unable to drive. A nice couple thankfully stopped us. They offered to drive our van back to the campsite. The only problem: We were way too intoxicated and disoriented for any of us to know the way back.

The nice couple just so happened to be housesitting their neighbors' cabin and let us crash there for the night. Unfortunately, we were in party mode and not ready to call it a night. We were up late and managed to trash the cabin. One guy fell, hitting his head on the coffee table, leaving a small pool of blood, and someone else vomited all over the place. Another guy pissed all over the floor 'cause he couldn't find the bathroom.

After passing out for a few hours, we awoke and felt the need to get the hell out of there. It was six in the morning. That sweet couple who saved us was still sound asleep, so we had to wake them to retrieve our keys. Rather than manning up and handling the situation responsibly, we ran—a rather immature thing to do, but we were still drunk. Returning to the camp, we quickly packed up our things and left the island, almost certain they would be waiting for us at the ferry. We *trashed* that cabin, leaving blood, piss, and vomit on the floor. We assumed the worst if they were to see us again.

The next year, many of "the boys" found themselves in serious relationships and were beginning to settle down. I like to blame the girls for locking them down, but I'm pretty sure it wasn't the ladies holding them back. We were all in our thirties (one of us was even in his forties), and we were growing old and tired of that life on the road. Being dirty skate punks had lost its appeal. Even if skateboarding would always be a lifelong obsession, wanting to settle down is natural. I was still a skateboarder for a few years afterward. However, I finally decided to give it up for my own kind of committed relationship: to becoming a chef. I wasn't after the typical family life; instead, I felt love, passion, and purpose in the kitchen. It was time to be not just a half-ass chef. I wanted to be fully committed. I wanted to become a real chef.

Part of the chef culture was finally participating in Vendetta's legendary Lake Powell trip.

Every spring, Vendetta's planned an employee vacation to Lake Powell on the Utah/Arizona border. The vacation was a celebration for an amazing, successful, and usually long season. Popeye would pay for the entire trip as a way of thanking his staff for their hard work. Long winters would make everyone crave a little warm weather, and a mere six-hour drive from Vail there was an oasis. An oasis often described as the Grand Canyon filled with water. Our payback to Popeye was that the veterans of the trip would do all the planning. This was Popeye's vacation, too, so it was only appropriate for us to allow him to relax.

The Vendetta's Lake Powell trip, which Popeye had been making since the eighties, had become legendary with Vail locals. Vendetta's had long known how to party. In the office, among many other photos, there was a large, twenty-inch blow-up of the entire staff during sunset on the rocky desert surrounding Lake Powell, which embodied the eccentric, wild attitude of the eighties lifestyle. They were a wild time, especially in a ski town in the western part of the country. Those were times I fantasized about; just like eighties glam bands, I envied the rock star lifestyle of those ski bums. Guys like Glen Plake and Jeff Brushie with their wild hair and bright neon jackets, simple symbols of a good time. With movies like Hot Dog that glamorized the party lifestyle of Olympic skiers in Squaw Valley, how could I not envy those times? Then here in the Vendetta's office, there sat an oversized photo of Vail locals having the time of their lives, the likes of which I had only seen in movies, magazines, and documentaries.

Although it was an experience that I fantasized about, the stories I heard were intimidating. They were mainly stories of sex and often heavy drug use. I was hesitant and nervous. My newly established coworkers were still strangers to me. I wasn't sure being stranded in the middle of a desert for a full week with thirty people I barely knew was a great idea.

I learned that being stuck in the desert with coworkers was exactly what I needed. The trip was possibly and passively conceived as a perfect team-building experiment. Every restaurant should adopt this type of team-building: a full week where everyone is forced to spend time together outside of work. There was nowhere to hide, and over the next five days, everyone's true personality eventually showed through. During a week away from the stress and pressure of the restaurant world, everyone from the owner to the busser, with the help of drugs and alcohol, learned to relax and let their guard down. There was never any judgment in the desert. Everyone was getting wrecked together.

Except "Straight Nate."

Straight Nate was a long-time pizza cook at Vendetta's and was aptly nicknamed "Straight," because he would never drink or do drugs. On these Lake Powell trips, we called him Captain. As the only one on the trip who would never be under the influence, he was always the designated driver. Although completely sober, Nate loved these trips.

The legendary stories that made it back to Vail were usually about parties; a good time is what most people want to boast about. However, there was so much more to Lake Powell than doing drugs in the desert. Simply canyon cruising was all one really needed. Lake Powell is a truly majestic place. Nate loved fireworks and would put on a good show at night, but I think his real passion was exploring, and he loved driving the boats. Vendetta's knew how to do things right. If someone didn't already own certain watercraft, we rented everything Lake Powell had to offer: multiple houseboats, ski boats, and jet skis. There was nothing we'd skimp on.

Although meant as an employee-only party, there were a few exceptions. A former cook at Vendetta's, Winger, who had gone on to work at many notable Vail restaurants, was invited on the trip with an agreement to prepare our daily meals. We essentially had a private chef, preparing amazing meals for us daily. Much of the prep work was done in the Vendetta's kitchen, allowing for more free time on the lake.

We purchased an enormous seventy-five-pound pig to be cooked Kalua (Hawaiian) style, reminiscent of what I had on my trip to Hawaii a few years earlier. Although we were not fully traditional, we planned our own luau on a rocky Lake Powell beach. The pig would provide enough meat to make sandwiches as snacks for the entirety of the trip. We stuffed the pig with pineapple and other aromatics and wrapped the hog with banana leaves held together with chicken wire. At our campsite, we began digging a giant hole; we were using traditional Kalua pig techniques. Ideally, the hole needed to be six-feet deep, deep enough to bury a human body. The ground, however, proved to be too hard. We only managed to dig a couple feet down, so we decided to build up the sides.

The next step was to build a giant fire. Not a problem for a bunch of pyros like me. The large fire was a necessity, because we needed to acquire two feet worth of coal—which became another failure. We were drunk, having a good time, and ran out of patience. We dropped the huge hog in our little hole and buried it. Kalua pig is a beautiful cooking technique, a process where you are cooking blind, unlike standard cooking techniques, where you are able to watch the whole process as it is happening. We had no idea what was going on under the mound of dirt and rocks.

It took us a few more tries before we could enjoy the true beauty of this technique. We utterly failed, hammering the pig and burning seventy percent of the meat. As it turned out, our hole had many flaws. Our hole wasn't a burial. The walls we built around our pit were made with a combination of large rocks and dirt. The large rocks created holes, which allowed too much oxygen, resulting in a burning fire rather than just hot coals. Our seventy-five-pound pig was charcoal.

Although our pig may have been a failure, the rest of our meals were spectacular. The last night of our trip was "Prom Night," complete with the crowning of a king and queen. Everyone dressed up, usually in a silly way. Dave, nicknamed Dark Pie or D.P. from burning many pizzas at the pizza bar, wore nothing but beer boxes one prom. Cross-dressing was also common, and I was guilty of wearing a dress for prom once or twice.

Along with dressing up, we also traditionally served surf and turf. Popeye loved his food, so there was no skimping on this meal. Steak and crab legs were our only option. Our chef, Winger, showed me the ideal way to portion a strip loin. I still knew little about food, and looking at the steaks on the grill, it looked like we were having filets. Inquiring with the chef, I learned that was intentional. Rather than cutting the loins into New Yorks, he had cut them into what is known as Manhattans, as they resemble the lower part of New York. Winger explained to me that the steaks cook up better that way. Rather than having a thin slice, we would have thick portions, allowing for more even cooking. Also known as a baseball cut, the steaks resembled filets.

Dinners were always well planned, and to keep everything fair, there was a schedule where everyone took turns either cooking or cleaning. With Lake Powell being a week-long party, having to cook or clean every night severely cut into our fun; with a schedule, our fun would only need to stop for one night the entire trip.

Additional to nightly "family meals," we had martini hour. Promptly at five o'clock every night, a large batch of traditional martinis would be made. Everyone was allowed to enjoy the refreshing cocktails; however, there was one very strict rule. Only those of us who were over thirty were allowed to enjoy olives with our martinis. This was a simple jest to keep the punk kids in their place. Everyone younger was deemed not worthy of an olive and only got cocktail onions. I was under thirty, and I assumed the veterans considered me to be less sophisticated, so I got an onion. Of course, if that was their assumption, they were right. I didn't know anything about martins. I just drank cheap beer and tequila.

With everyone gathered around on the top of the houseboat, it was time for the "ejector." The ski boat pulled two tubes, and the occupants battled each other with the goal to cause their opponent to "eject" into the air. The ejector became a competition for not only who could hold on the longest, but also who could eject the highest. To make the event even more exciting, we included a "trouble boat." One boat drove circles in the middle of the lake, creating a cyclone of crashing waves. Riding a tube, you have absolutely no control, and the pullboat dragged the helpless competitors at high speeds through the cyclone of death. It was inevitable that someone was about to go airborne. While most people volunteered to ride the ejector, for rookies such as myself, it was mandatory.

For most of the trip, I was paired up with this girl, Erin. We were the only rookies on this trip. We had been assigned the same carpool, so we rode to the lake together. After arriving at the lake, we stayed in the same hotel room before renting our boat in the morning. Back in the room, I remember watching her walk around the room in her underwear. Erin was sexy! I thought to myself. *I guess this is how these wild employee party orgies are going to start. We're just going to jump right into it.* But even with my hormones in a full rage, nothing ever happened between the two of us. It was the first night of our trip, and I still felt a little timid. I wasn't ready to fully engage in the sex and drugs that had been glamorized over the years. I felt like a nervous virgin all over again.

As rookies, it was an obvious choice for us to be paired up together for the ejector. It should also come as no surprise I easily lost the battle. I had, and still have, a severely bad shoulder. Trying to hold onto the tube proved to be impossible. I was unable to extend my arms, which would have kept the tube level. Using a crossed-arm technique, I quickly flipped, and the contest was over. I had, at least, fulfilled my obligation as a rookie to be ejected.

After a solid week together, strong bonds formed, and the Vendetta's team was stronger than ever. Although we may not have always gotten along, the good times negated any negatives we had with one another. Without the Lake Powell trips, I'm not sure how tight of a family we would have become. I learned how much everyone was willing to care for each other. Before my first trip, I was shy and scared to really open up. Afterward, life became a completely different story.

Traveling back to Vail from Lake Powell was a long struggle, as everyone was nursing the painful hangovers from the week-long binge. It's unfortunate how all good times must end, but it was time to return back to work. After returning the houseboat, we loaded up all our gear in our separate cars and prepared for the long journey home. The six-hour drive seemed like eternity. As we eased our way back into reality, there was always one more mandatory stop: Stan's Burger Shack in Hanksville, Utah. We enjoyed amazing burgers and shakes, knowing this would be the last time our team would be together as happy vaca-tioners. Until next year's Powell trip.

Skate crew, ferry ride to orcas

Our campsite on Orcas
with the essentials

Packing the van, somewhere in Idaho

Drinking in the Newberg parking lot,
Oregon

The karaoke girls outside our hotel on the streets of Manila

At the snowboarding world championships with "The Godmother of Snowboarding" Tina Basich

The Vendetta's family in Minneapolis for Danny's wedding

In the Vendetta's kitchen' prepping the pig
for Lake Powell

With the king, celebrating
as royalty

Team Vendetta's, Lake Powell

# Chapter 10:

## The Unconventional Route to Becoming a Chef

The Pippen and Paul Shit Show days were a thing of the past. I had a new crew of delinquents. Scooby and Ferg had just joined our team. Aside from my skate crew, Scoob and Ferg were two of my best friends. We had known each other for years, wreaking havoc wherever we went; we were trouble. Vail's drunk tank had affectionately become known as the "Ferg Inn," a place where Ferg was a near permanent fixture. I learned from firsthand experience at the Ferg Inn to be sure to ask for an extra blanket to use as a pillow, as such a luxury would not be provided.

Ferg was quite the character, truly living a unique life all of his own—including a tattoo across his stomach that read "Ferg Life," emulating Tupac's "Thug Life" tattoo. Unlike Tupac, however, Ferg was no thug. He just didn't handle his booze very gracefully. He even created his own drop shot, the Ferg Bomb: your cheapest shot of whiskey dropped into your cheapest beer. I don't recommend it. However, the Ferg Bomb inspired me to make my own signature bomb, the Asian Bomb. Not to be confused with a sake bomb, an Asian Bomb was my two favorites put together: a shot of Sauza Hornitos Reposado dropped into a Miller High Life. They really toughen you up! If you don't instantly vomit, you can handle anything. I liked to try talking people into trying one by telling them they tasted like vanilla. "It'll be the next big thing to sweep the nation. You'll be hearing about them on MSNBC."

Although true delinquents, Scoob and Ferg were both capable cooks, having worked in the industry for several years by this point. Although we loved to party, when it came to cooking, we had a strong crew that was capable of weathering through the toughest of services. Three hundred covers? We got this. Not a problem.

Our bar manager was Dave, more commonly known by his nickname, Bone. He'd worked with Popeye since the early years, so Popeye made him part-owner of the restaurant. In addition to being involved with the restaurant, Bone was also well into politics and ended up becoming the mayor of Vail. Bone was always a generous man who, in addition to caring about his community, also took excellent care of his staff.

Every time the liquor or beer reps brought in free samples, Bone delivered them to the kitchen, saying, "Here, I'm sure you guys can figure out something to do with these." We'd return a smile and say, "Thanks, Bone." Surely, we could find something to do with those three cases of Bud Light Lime.

Beer and liquor companies often experiment with new flavors and products, and as marketing, the products are delivered to bars to gauge the market. Many businesses will attempt to sell the free product, and at even low "special" prices, they still make money. Bone, however, was more like, "Fuck that. Give it to the kitchen. They'll drink anything." He was pretty much right. Whatever weird new flavor was, for the most part, better than the warm house wine from a box that we were using for cooking. Bone always took exceptional care of the kitchen staff, thanking us with free booze for all our hard work. We were strong cooks, and also big alcoholics.

Our dining room was located below street level, so we had no windows and it was out of public view. Often on busy, late nights, we held after-hour parties with only our friends. It was illegal to serve alcohol after two in the morning in Colorado, but with no windows, we could easily have a private party.

One night, I was walking home from one of our late-night dance parties when I was approached by two police officers. They asked me about a fight that had broken out in front of another bar. I told them I had no idea what they were talking about, because I had been at Vendetta's the whole night. I told them the truth. As I turned and continued to walk home, with my back turned to the police, I was tased twice in the back. With the electrical current running through my body, I was tackled to the ground. The cop then pressed his knee into my back and placed me in handcuffs. During my booking, they had me take off my shirt for photos, showing burn marks on my back from the tasers and a bruised sternum.

As I lay in the jail cell, the two arresting officers frequently looked into the cell and laughed at me, as I was helpless. Words can't describe how infuriated I was. I had done nothing wrong. Both officers were bigger than me—one of the officers was stocky and the other was simply a big bitch—yet they used excessive force to take me down. I thought it was a clear sign of power tripping. This event furthered my distrust and hatred toward the police.

When I arrived for my court date to argue my defense for being charged with resisting arrest, I went through the arrest report with the district attorney. While reading the report, we noticed an obvious sign of misconduct. The report stated that "the suspect in the fight was a dark-skinned guy wearing a brown hoodie." I was wearing a grey hoodie. It also stated that I had been tased twice in the back. Before the district attorney got much further reading the report, he quickly decided to drop the charges as a clear case of racial profiling.

Although we may have been heavy alcoholics who liked to party, we were still close friends and good cooks. Because of this, I was capable of being more ambitious with my specials. I could always trust my team to finish setting up and prepping their stations; they would always be prepared for service. I was still very much developing as a chef, but my dishes were something I was becoming proud of. For the first time in my life, I had one of my dishes officially put on the menu. Vendetta's was advertised as "Northern Italian," so I researched what was considered Northern Italian food. I learned they specialize in serving more rice rather than pasta. I created a fish dish served over saffron risotto with what I was calling a tomato beurre blanc. I delivered the dish to Popeye and the other managers for a tasting. Popeye put it on the menu. Having my own creation on a menu was a big milestone.

We kept the team of Joe, Scoob, Ferg, and me together for quite a few years before we dramatically split. Simply put and without the details, we had become too comfortable in our kitchen, and our alcoholic ways caught up to us. It was just time for Scoob and Ferg to move on. Joe and I were the last two to survive another major staff turnover.

Scoob and Ferg were then replaced by another good friend, Danny. He was a recovering heroin addict. After spending some time in jail, he was now clean, at least when it came to heroin.

I'm not sure if it was narcolepsy or bourbon—he loved his Wild Turkey—but he often passed out in bars. Bar owners generally frowned upon unconscious patrons. Danny, however, was a regular, and often the owners would look the other way. I loved Danny; he was probably the hardest worker I have ever seen in my life and a capable cook who was always prepared for service. He was somewhat of a surprising idiot savant and could do crossword puzzles like nothing I had ever seen. With the new addition of Danny, Joe and I once again had a strong team.

During this time, I also met the most encouraging and influential girl of my life, Angelee, an accomplished chef—although the night we met, I had no idea that she even was a chef. That night, I was feeling really good, and by that, I mean it was my day off so I had been drinking for quite a while. Scooby and I were standing at the bar. I glanced to my right, and saw the most beautiful hazel eyes with smokey eyeliner. The girl ordered a drink, I asked the bartender to put it on my tab, and we struck up a conversation.

She began, "I have really big boobs."

I replied, "I'm more of an ass man."

She turned around to show (and offer) me her butt, so I gave it a quick squeeze. She had a great butt, too. As the conversation continued, I asked the bartender for some paper so we could exchange numbers. I still liked the old-school feeling of a handwritten note. It just seemed more personal. After exchanging numbers, her friend chimed in, saying they were going to a club to dance and asked if I wanted to join. I was well into the double digits of tequila shots, so I declined—almost certain I would fuck up my currently good situation.

A few days passed, maybe even a full week, when Scooby

ran into Angelee at a free concert. When I saw Scooby the next day, he said, "Dude, seriously, you gotta call her."

Angelee was smoking hot. Intelligent, too. She was the perfect package. Tequila had given me the liquid courage to bravely approach her at the bar, but sober, I was all fear. I had never really been into dating. But how could I let a girl this good go?

Considering Scoob was such a good friend, I took his advice and gave Angelee a call, despite my nerves. When I called her up, I could hear conversations in the background. One of the things I could hear was, "Ask him how old he is?" Obviously my age was in question. Angelee was older than me, but not by much. However, she was clearly more experienced, and by that, I mean in life in general. I later learned she had worked in a Michelin-starred restaurant in France and was fluent in French. She was also previously employed as the executive chef at the French Press and currently owned her own catering company, Amuse Bouche. Was she out of my league? Possibly. Had I known any of that, I'm not quite sure I would have had the balls to do what I did next: ask her out.

I hadn't been on a date in years, and truthfully, I would say I had never been on a real, "adult-style," intimate date like a nice dinner. But the way Scoob had put it seemed as though I absolutely had to go out with her or I was a fucking idiot. So after she agreed to go on a date with me, I arranged reservations at a restaurant called Terra Bistro. After the date was set, I felt really uncomfortable. *Am I really going to do this? Why can't we just do the casual let's-just-go-snowboarding-together kinda date? The kind of date most of my friends would do in the mountains. What was I thinking?*

The day of our date, I was nervous and tried not to think

about it, so naturally I ended up at the skate park. Skateboarding would relax me. It was what I was most comfortable with. As the time of our reservation was approaching, I was still at the skate park. I thought to myself, *Shit. Remember when you stood up Tina Basich?* I'd already fucked up once. I wasn't going to stand up Angelee.

So I left the skate park. I took a quick sink shower at Vendetta's and, still wearing shorts and a torn, sweaty T-shirt, I met up with Angelee. She looked gorgeous in her black dress. She saw me and gave me the exact same look that Tina Basich had given me several years earlier; she raised hand her hands like "What the fuck?" I thought to myself, *Sorry! But hey, at least I showed up this time.* I was putting forth at least a little effort to become a more mature, respectable adult—attempting to put my misfit, punk lifestyle behind me. Although I wasn't dressed appropriately, we managed to still have a great dinner. Angelee turned out to be amazingly good company. I am thankful to still call her a friend, as she continues to be my greatest supporter. I'm just sorry I wasn't dressed better for our first date.

Meanwhile back at Vendetta's, we continued to have a strong team, and I became completely comfortable creating specials. My ambitions had become so great I was actually beginning to prep components days in advance. I made potato gnocchi from scratch; even with no true plan, I would just freeze them for a later purpose. Sauces could also hold for days. Vinaigrettes became a favorite of mine to serve with fish, gastriques for meat dishes. My culinary repertoire was starting to grow. I was fully beginning to embrace my opportunity to express myself through my food and gaining confidence to trust my own palate.

I was beginning to become more dedicated to my work, and

successful dinner services became a priority. While Joe, Danny, and I were close friends and the leaders of our kitchen, we still had plenty of F.N.G.s passing through our kitchen. Al was an older guy who had plenty of experience in the industry, but to us, he was still the fucking new guy. Al knew what he was doing, but one day he was taking too long to set up his station. Although I understood he was busy, I didn't like how he was prioritizing his time. At one point, I was looking for him because I was curious what he was up to. When I found Al, he was in the back prep room using our deli slicer. He was prepping his station, but I was already too fired up and prepared to yell at him. There was no holding me back at this point, and I went off on him. The argument resulted in Al saying "Fuck this" and walking out. He never returned to work.

For the most part, I had confidence in our staff. However, my commitment to a successful service brought on added stress that I was still learning to deal with. One day while prepping my station, I looked around and didn't see much of my staff. I assumed they were just socializing at the bar. Whether it was justified or not, I felt I was the only one committed to a successful service. I lost my composure and screamed a few cuss words, making a scene, and walked out. I needed a break to cool off a little bit. After I walked a few laps through the village, I regained my cool and returned to work. There, I was happy to see my entire staff was back in the kitchen prepared for service.

After being gifted David Walford's *Wood Fire and Champagne Powder,* I was hooked on cookbooks, but not just any cookbooks. I was hooked on the best chefs in the world. Thomas Keller's *The French Laundry Cookbook* was one of my first, followed by many other notable chefs, such as Éric Ripert and

Grant Achatz. I couldn't get enough of a vision of what some of the best restaurants in the world were serving. I began reading novels from legendary chefs, memoirs of their journeys. I read Anthony Bourdain's *Kitchen Confidential: Adventures in the Culinary Underbelly*. Before, I was never into books and hated school. I lacked the patience and focus to actually finish a book. But with Kitchen Confidential, I finished it with ease. Bourdain was not a trailblazing, world-renowned chef. Rather, his story was one I could relate to. Bourdain wrote with a raw, unfiltered style, showing no fear of what the public or other industry leaders would think. His story felt familiar: the degenerates and the valuable Mexican porters. It was true that the industry would fail without them. Drug use is rampant in the industry, especially cocaine—doing key bumps in the walk-in every hour during service, just to get through the rush. Key bumps were a convenient way to get a quick burst of energy. No mirrors, credit cards, or rolled-up dollar bills were needed. Just dip a key in the bag, put the tip of the key to your nose, and sniff. It was as simple as that.

In fact, early on at Vendetta's, there were several police raids on the restaurant. Two of our employees at the pizza bar were selling cocaine. Although the illegal transactions were not directly associated with the restaurant, someone had ratted them out as to where they worked. There had been a long-going sting throughout Vail in an attempt to reduce the rampant drug use. Several of my friends were ultimately busted and given jail time. Cocaine became increasingly hard to find and risky to possess. Popeye would undoubtably attempt to "rip our fucking heads off" if he caught us doing cocaine on his property after the raids.

This also happened to be around the time Red Bull energy drinks burst onto the scene. Although the beverages were legal, I questioned the health risks. During the Pippen and Paul Shit Show Era, we all but abandoned the cocaine key bumps for shotgunning Red Bulls. Poking a hole in the side of the can created a funneling effect, increasing our consumption rate. Talk about getting your heart going. Those little key bumps didn't compare to the rush of Red Bull.

For me, *Kitchen Confidential* was such a good read that I read the book multiple times. In the book, Bourdain mentioned a chef by the name of Marco Pierre White. I had never heard of Marco Pierre White at the time, but by Bourdain's accounts, White blew the doors off the industry long before *Kitchen Confidential* was published. White's cookbook, *White Heat*, showing the unglamorous work of creating Michelin star food, had inspired Bourdain's staff during his time at Les Halles in New York. White had also written his own memoir, *The Devil in the Kitchen: Sex, Pain, Madness, and the Making of a Great Chef.* Bourdain recommended the book as a must-read.

Taking Bourdain's advice, I ordered the book off Amazon, and The Devil in the Kitchen became by far the most inspirational read of my life. White's story was told in the most humbling way possible, very unlike most celebrity chefs. At the time, White was the youngest chef to achieve the Michelin Guide's highest rating of three stars and the first chef to famously "return" his stars. A groundbreaking chef with a humble beginning. Bourdain had given me a story of a life that I was already living, and then there was Marco Pierre White telling me a story of how my life could become.

My old friend, Scooby, had left Vendetta's, moving on to work in the Manor Vail Lodge at its contemporary Lord Gore Restaurant. Lord Gore's dining room had probably the best views in all of Vail: a large, fully glass wall overlooking snow-covered Golden Peak. With a large fireplace, it had the perfect ambiance. Marco Pierre White had become my idol, and his achievement became my goal. Toward the end of White's journey to achieve Michelin star greatness, he raved of his dining room with tall ceilings and large chandeliers. The grandness of how I envisioned White's three-Michelin-star dining room was found at the Manor Vail.

Inspired by White, I gave Vendetta's a month-long notice after about five years of employment. I figured I had become such an important piece of the restaurant that a month rather than the standard two weeks was appropriate. When my notice was over, I joined Scooby in Lord Gore's glamorous dining room. However, my absence from Vendetta's was short-lived. Within two weeks, I began suffering from extreme insomnia and was experiencing a weird vertigo feeling. My mental status was unnerving. After meeting with Lord Gore's chef and manager, they said they felt I was not quite ready to leave Vendetta's.

I returned to Vendetta's, and Rafa offered me my old position in his kitchen once again. The chef at Lord Gore had been right. I wasn't ready to leave. Not yet. I was happy to see that nothing had changed, including my locker. During my short time at Lord Gore, I had a realization: No matter how grand the dining room or the appearance of a restaurant, when it comes down to it, all kitchens are virtually the same.

I was back in my familiar kitchen doing what I truly loved: creating my own personal dishes, learning on my own, and having complete freedom. I knew I was taking an unconventional route to become a chef, but that had always been my way. Without a title, I was still my own boss. I also think on some level, Vendetta's still needed me. With our thirtieth anniversary now in the horizon, Popeye yet again had big plans, bigger than the huge bash he had thrown a few years earlier. Popeye had plans to close the restaurant for a few months so it could undergo a major expansion.

Next to Vendetta's was a small toy store and just past the toy store was a candy shop. Popeye planned to expand the pizza bar by another sixty seats, moving into the toy store and a third of the candy store. Vendetta's was about to take over Bridge Street. Up until now, our pizza bar was tiny, really just an after-thought. But over the years, the quick and convenient street-side bar had become our main focus and identity, and our biggest money-maker. Our old, small, three-level oven could no longer keep up with the demand. Often, guests had to wait an hour or longer for pizza. Table turnover was slow to say the least. We figured new, larger ovens could solve the problem.

Because of inspectors and other unexpected problems, our grand re-opening was continuously being pushed back farther and farther. Major construction projects such as this always take longer than expected, but this project seemed never ending. When we finally decided the construction was close enough, we set our official opening date. We were still laying plywood and not even thinking of the carpet yet. With the bar and the floor unfinished, we decided to begin advertising. It was Monday, not even a week until we needed to officially be ready for our grand opening that Friday evening. It was not nearly enough time for the amount of work required, not to mention we still needed to restock the bar and put away a massive food order.

Luckily, our staff was eager to get back to work, so we had a team willing to work around the clock. We cooks chipped in however we could. We were as excited as anyone. And when

Friday finally came around, we were working as late as possible. With a large gathering of patrons on our patio and at our front door, Popeye asked, "Are the taps working? Is there money in the registers?" Our answer:

"Sure!" With railings freestanding, screwing things down was not a priority, and with wet paint on the walls, we opened the door. Although we were only serving beverages, after waiting months, our regulars were pleased they could finally get their Vendetta's fix.

The expansion wasn't our only project, though. Although our kitchen wasn't expanding, we got some great upgrades to our equipment. Particularly our new ovens and a new four-teen-burner, 40,000-BTU stove. Normal commercial ranges are only around 30,000 BTUs. Our stove was hot—and in perfect condition.

In addition to our appliances, we got a new floor installed. A top-notch material, spongy and non-slip. No mats were neces-sary, and it was nearly indestructible. The floors were a dream for a commercial kitchen—fully sealed and easy to clean. Our health inspector also loved them. The only catch: Only one com-pany in the country installed them, located on the east coast, and these floors were not cheap. The kitchen took a little more time to complete, but when we finally finished, business was booming. No, that's an understatement. Our seating capacity had grown considerably, however our kitchen had stayed the same size. Although services eventually settled down, I remem-ber one occasion staring at twelve feet worth of tickets. We were beyond over our heads, and our ship was sinking hard and fast. Even with the upgrades in the pizza bar, the extra seating still made it challenging to keep the ticket times down. The question now became: What would be next for Vendetta's? How far could Popeye take it?

We finished the expansion just in time for ski season. As it turned out, this would be my last winter at Vendetta's. I may have subconsciously known it would be my last. Internally, I felt my work was finally done. In a nearly ten-year span, I had witnessed a remodel followed by a massive expansion. Upon our reopening, Popeye was in the wine room taking inventory when I approached him and asked for a raise. Probably not the best timing, considering he just spent nearly half a million dollars on the restaurant, but I felt I was worth more. To my pleasant surprise, Popeye not only agreed to pay me my requested raise, but he also upped my offer, paying me more than I had asked.

During the same informal meeting, I asked Popeye if he would mind if we only served one special each night. Up until now, we had been serving two specials a night: one meat and one fish. I told Popeye that I would like to be even more ambitious with my dishes. By cutting back my work from two dishes to one, I had more focus and this feat was more feasible. Popeye agreed.

When the season began, I decided to challenge myself. I wanted to never serve the exact same dish more than once for the entire winter. By the time April rolled around, I had succeeded.

Around this time, a new kid, Christian, joined the Vendetta's team. Christian had recently returned from the Northeast, having worked fine dining in the New England area. At only twenty-two years old, Christian already had experience and ambition. I could sense Christian was preparing to take over my position, just as I had prepared to take over for Danny nearly ten years earlier.

One day, I went to pick up my paycheck from the office. It was in the drawer on top of the stack. Christian had just left the office. It was obvious he had peeked at my check to see how much I was making. A few days later, Christian asked me about my ski pass. I felt I had nothing to hide, nor was I trying to boast or brag. However, I knew my days at Vendetta's were now numbered. So I let him know that Popeye was also paying for my pass. I realized, looking back, that I had inadvertently put Popeye in a bad situation, while additionally creating resentment between me and Christian. The information should have been kept private. As soon as the words left my mouth, I knew I had made a mistake.

Springtime came around. It was once again time for the annual Vendetta's employee party in the desert. On the lake, the usual shenanigans occurred. The rampant drug use was more apparent than ever. In previous years, drugs were primarily confined to our tents. Now, drug use was more open. Scarface-sized piles of cocaine sat on the dining room table—situations that were simply not cool. It had gone too far. Although it was outside of the confines of Vendetta's legally-bound walls, this was still a Vendetta's party. A ranger could walk onto that boat at any time. Copious amounts of cocaine in the open was risky and disrespectful to Popeye and the rest of the "family."

However, the stories of our ragers on the lake had become legendary. Because the storytelling had become so open, the new generation believed that was how these trips to the lake had always been. On the first day of the trip this summer, I took psychedelic mushrooms. That was when I realized I was past that stage of my life. I preferred sitting back and watching the others get fucked up and trip. I was now the veteran.

Although Vendetta's had previously taken a break from this traditional celebration, this trip would prove to be not only my last trip to Lake Powell but also the restaurant's. It seemed like the end of an era. Vendetta's was beginning to pass the torch to a new generation.

In my early years, I had wondered how someone else had always been there to take care of me. I was a constant disaster on the trips, like many of the other people. I figured everyone had been as constantly fucked up as I was. Now I was maturing, at least a little, and my perspective was changing. Just the previous year, I had been voted the prom queen. Yes, queen. In a hot pink dress, I was the most popular "girl" at the prom. This year, a new queen was to be crowned. The new royal couple was the newlyweds, Emily and Ricky. The passing of my crown was also symbolically the passing of the torch. I was almost certainly leaving Vendetta's. It was time for me to move on.

# Chapter II:

## Eating My Way Through Europe

At Vendetta's, I met a girl from Sweden named Rebecca, although I never called her that. To me, she was "The Hippie." The Hippie was one of the most laid-back people I had ever met. She loved weed and liked to run on what I called "hippie time." While some people might be fashionably late, she casually showed up whenever, at least twenty minutes late.

The Hippie knew about my dedication to becoming a chef. One night I was drinking with her at a bar when she informed me that she grew up just a short train ride from one of the best restaurants in the world, Noma. Noma in Copenhagen had been named the best restaurant in the world for four years by the San Pellegrino World's 50 Best Restaurant list (back when restaurants could be named the best more than once). So, when she told me her brother was getting married that summer, I asked her if I could be her plus one. She said sure. Since we were drunk in a bar, naturally she didn't take me too seriously. I'd essentially invited myself to her brother's wedding. But I wasn't kidding. As the months passed by, I kept reminding her I was going to fly with her to Sweden. First, I needed to apply for a new passport. I sent her a text when my passport arrived, and she finally started to believe me.

I was driven by the curiosity of what all the hype was about.

Was Noma really deserving of the title best restaurant in the *world*? I felt an overwhelming urge; I needed to find out for myself. So, I called up my old friend Danny. He had worked at Noma for six months, and he described his experience as "I'm best friends with the sous chef and all we do is forage during the day, then do a bunch of coke, and chase girls every night." Regardless of his description, I asked him if he could get me a seat. His response: "Sure, not a problem."

But as it turned out, Noma would be closed during my entire visit. I already had the tickets, so now I needed a new plan. After further research, I came across Geranium. I had never heard of this restaurant before. This was during a time when every restaurant, especially Nordic restaurants, were chasing after Noma as the leader of the pack. Geranium's head chef and own-er was Rasmus Kofoed, another chef I had never heard of at the time. I didn't know of him because he was chasing a separate goal. He wanted Bocuse d'Or gold, an honor created by legend-ary French chef Paul Bocuse and held in his hometown of Lyon, France. The Bocuse d'Or is globally recognized as the ultimate showcase of culinary skill, and often referred to as the "Culi-nary Olympics," as it's only held every two years with only one team from each country allowed to compete. After nine years of competing in the most prestigious culinary competition in the world, Rasmus had finally achieved his goal. After first winning the bronze, silver and gold medals quickly followed. At the time, no American chef had won a single medal.

I became extremely intrigued by this new, up-and-coming chef. Although well-known in Europe for his achievements, he had yet to make a name for himself in the states, much less in the global scene. I decided to make a booking for Geranium.

Bookings were only open up two months in advance and filled up quickly. The Hippie declined the offer to join me; she had too many personal things to take care of, along with preparing for the wedding. So I booked a reservation for just one. I booked an early seating, lunchtime, so I could explore the city during the evening. Geranium offered no menu. Just two simple options: a two-hour meal or a three-hour meal with beverage pairings optional. With no other options, I assumed it wouldn't matter whether I ate there for lunch or dinner.

My main priority of the trip had finally been planned. I was officially flying across the pond to eat. A Michelin-starred restaurant was in my sights. My only thought now was how in the hell was I going to afford this trip?

Many years earlier, I had decided to finally build up my credit. Credit was something I knew nearly nothing about, however I knew I had bad credit as a result of unpaid medical bills, from my younger snowboarder bum days. Using my limited knowledge about credit, I figured the easiest way to build credit was to use credit cards. As I paid them off in full, it should work on developing a better financial standing. My first credit card had a minuscule $350 credit limit, but by now, my credit limit had reached $4,000. I thought surely that would be enough. But just to be safe, I got a second credit card. I figured since I hadn't built up a huge amount of college debt like most of my friends had, this might as well be my "college debt." I was studying food in my own way. The Hippie and I booked our $1,300 flights, and we were set.

Except we soon realized our trip was not yet fully planned. The Hippie's parents had been separated for some time, and along with their new partners, they owned property all over Europe. If we were going to fly all the way across the Atlantic, we decided we might as well explore as much of the continent as possible.

The Hippie's parents had properties in Croatia, Switzerland, and even a vineyard in the south of France. Not to mention, she also had a good friend living in Amsterdam who we could stay with. My love for the beach made Croatia a top priority. With a beach house on the island of Hvar, my visions of paradise were well within reach. We knew we didn't have enough time to visit all these amazing destinations, so the planning proved to be quite difficult. We managed to get the best deals by booking all our flights separately. It took months of searching flights, but now we finally had our full itinerary. Although the vineyard in France was high on my list, the nearest airport was small, which resulted in limited flights and unaffordable prices. Skipping out on Amsterdam and France, we settled on Switzerland and Croatia. The Hippie and I finally had our trip planned and fully booked.

I was back to work at Vendetta's, but my mind and dedication were definitely not there. I had put in my request for the vacation time, but I had serious doubts I would be returning to Vendetta's after Europe.

In the midst of planning our trip, we had a costing meeting for our new menu at Vendetta's. The meeting occurred on my day off, and I decided to skip the meeting and focus on planning my trip. The following day, I got a phone call from Joe; we had worked together for a decade now, and it was only appropriate for him to give me the news that they were letting me go. Unlike previously when I had given a full month's notice, everyone knew it was time for me to move on.

This time I was prepared. I didn't need to wait weeks to return and empty out my locker. I cleared it out the next day. Filled with more excitement than uncertainty, I couldn't wait to leave for Europe. I kept thinking back on when I was happiest; I wasn't happy at Vendetta's anymore. I thought about my first few years in Vail—how I had dropped out of school, packed my car, and driven to Colorado. Those were exciting times. I'd loved the feeling of uncertainty and adventure. The unknown.

Now I was officially out of work. I had free time to enjoy Vail again. It was amazing how much Vail had changed. I went to a free concert at the Ford Amphitheater. These concerts had been in their infancy when I first arrived in Vail. In my early twenties, we often attended the free shows, tossing our cases of beer over the fence to avoid the high concession stand prices. Things had changed: much bigger crowds, increased security, and a taller fence where the shrubs had now become fully grown. It was virtually impossible to sneak in beer now. The concert crowds consisted of good-looking families—not dirty skaters like me back in the day, dripping in sweat with holes in my shirt. Even the local skaters at the shows seemed as if they had driven in, rather than skated in from the park. The concerts had a completely different feel from what I remembered.

Long gone were the days where Vail was chasing down Aspen for global resort supremacy. It seemed like Vail had surpassed Aspen. Aspen had developed a bitterness toward Vail; just take a day trip to Aspen and say you're from Vail, and you'd feel it. But in Vail, Aspen was almost never spoken of. Our heated, cobblestone streets, a true sign of luxury. The days of carrying all our gear from the bus to the lifts through three feet of snow were over. Our high-end guests no longer even had to carry their own gear. Ski valets with ski racks attached to bikes were now willing to shuttle your equipment directly to the lifts.

My greatest revelation, however, was the Fourth of July. One of Vail's busiest days of the year also happened to be Joe's birthday. I had not had the holiday off in a decade. The festivities stretched all over our village, complete with a family-friendly kids' zone, a parade stretching between Lionshead to Vail Village, cheerful families lining the streets, candy thrown, and little kids fearlessly running into the streets, a simple reminder of my childhood growing up in tiny Jackson. I missed those simple times.

Vail was my home, and as I had watched Vail grow, I had grown with Vail, as well. I wasn't the young, degenerate snowboard bum any longer. Vail as a town had matured, just as I had.

By mid-July, my new, exciting journey was set to begin. The Hippie and I booked a shuttle to the Denver airport. Our ten-hour flight had a short layover in Germany, where my fresh passport received its first stamp, before we finally arrived in Copenhagen in the early evening. Once we gathered our bags, we boarded a train on our way to Sweden. In Helsingborg, we walked around, and The Hippie showed me the beauty of the North Harbor. We met her mom at a local restaurant, but we didn't stay long, as we were tired from traveling.

The restaurant's bread was served with butter laced with shaved black truffles. This was the first time I had encountered the luxury ingredient. We were staying in the house that The Hippie had grown up in, and most of the time the house was vacant. So for the most part, we had the house to ourselves, with the exception of a few other wedding guests. I had my own room so I could enjoy the most privacy, and the next day I was to travel solo back to Denmark. Although I was exhausted, my excitement wouldn't let my body get a meaningful amount of sleep. I awoke at around seven in the morning. I was wide awake and anxious, with complete uncertainty about how to get back to Copenhagen, much less how to find the restaurant.

The Hippie and I had taken the train from the airport the previous night, however she informed me about a ferry that could take me to the other side of the North Sea. I decided I wanted a new adventure and to take the ferry. I will always love the open sea. For me, there is a more majestic feel that the train couldn't provide. It was only a short distance, but the train traveled through a tunnel, eliminating all scenery. I wanted to see some views! On the ferry, along with the open sea, you could see the Kronborg Castle, the castle that Shakespeare had made famous in his play *Hamlet*.

I wasn't much into using maps, nor did I own a smartphone yet, so I was under the impression that the ferry would take me all the way to Copenhagen. I was wrong. As we arrived at a train station somewhere in Denmark, I still hadn't looked at a map. So I asked directions from an attendant who spoke broken English. Her English was at least light years better than my completely nonexistent Danish. After receiving the instructions and purchasing my ticket, I boarded a train. We passed by many stops, before we finally stopped, and I saw the majority of the passengers exiting the train. I asked the same attendant if it was my stop. She seemed rather irritated by me, but said, "Yes, I already told you this." I walked off thinking, *"Well, thanks, lady."*

Copenhagen's train station is ideally located in a bustling part of the city. Thousands of people were casually commuting on the streets. As I left the station, I still had no idea where I was going or how I was going to find the restaurant. I didn't have any internet access, and not owning a smartphone was beginning to be a big dilemma. Although I still owned an old-school flip phone, I hadn't bothered contacting my service company to update my plan for global travel. I thought I would prefer it that way. I wanted the simple life of no cell phones. I decided to walk into a nearby hotel and ask for directions. Luckily, the front desk agent spoke perfect English. However, even with Michelin stars to its credit, the agent hadn't heard of Geranium.

I had been long infatuated with restaurant industry leaders, and although I had just recently learned of Geranium, I figured in this man's hometown, the hotel attendant should know of this gastronomical temple. Luckily, I had written down the address, an easy address that everyone in Copenhagen could find. Geranium is located on the eighth floor of the national soccer stadium. Not exactly the type of location you would expect to find a fine dining establishment. After I pointed to the address in my notebook, because it was Danish and I couldn't pronounce it, the agent said, "Ooh, that's kinda far." I responded, "That's fine. I've got all day." Although I had an early reservation, because I had gotten up at 7 a.m., I figured I still had plenty of time. Since it was a hotel, the helpful agent had a stack of convenient maps for this exact type of situation. He kindly handed me a map and drew out the exact route for me to take to get to the stadium.

After walking around the stadium, I finally found the elevators that would bring me to Geranium. Only the elevators were not in operation. I walked into the nearby business office to inquire. I was politely informed that the restaurant was not yet open. I asked the helpful worker what time it was, as I didn't own a watch or even a functioning cell phone, so I had no clue. I still had about a half hour. I waited in the park for what felt like fifteen minutes or so, checked the elevator again, but it was still not working. I tried several more times and finally had success.

Upon arriving at the host stand, the greeter offered to take my large backpack and place it in the coat room. I handed it over and explained to be careful, because I had my large digital camera with interchangeable lenses in it. He double-checked with me multiple times, making sure I didn't want the camera to take pictures of the food. The restaurant actually encouraged taking photos. Strongly. But I still felt old-school, envisioning a quiet, refined, pretentious restaurant. I thought stopping to take photos would disrupt the service. Besides that, I always loved the mysteriousness of restaurants of this caliber. If you wanted to experience the food, you had no choice but to actually spend the money and make the journey yourself.

I was seated at a table overlooking the kitchen. Through its large glass doors, I was close enough to hear the chef call out the tickets. Once seated, I was greeted with a note welcoming me to their "gastronomic universe." At the end of the note it said, "If you have any questions, please ask. We have no secrets." It was a warmhearted note.

I opted for the three-hour meal. Dishes came pouring out of the kitchen, one after the other. The first seven dishes were considered "snacks" or small bites. By the eighth course, the server brought out the setup for my expected next course. The server then returned to my table and removed the setup. "Sorry, not ready for this course yet," he said. It was a simple mistake, I understand, but the smallest of gestures proved to me that they were not perfect. Somewhere along the lines, there was some miscommunication. Was I eating too fast? Did the next course need more time to prepare? I didn't know, but I received a "bonus dish:" an oyster with fish skin and fermented cabbage. The server was unaware of the additional dish I got.

By the middle of the meal, the chef de cuisine came to my table and invited me into the kitchen to enjoy my next course. As I walked into the kitchen, I was welcomed with the warm smile of a cute, young cook in glasses. Geranium has a very international staff, and the restaurant takes pride in that. While my server was from France, this young cook was Italian. As she spoke to me in perfect English, she welcomed me into the Geranium kitchen, but she didn't need to say a word. Her smile was all I needed. I could tell she loved her job.

I was blown away by how happy everyone appeared. Chefs often focus on the pressures and stress of cooking, but there I was witnessing a happy staff. Not only were they happy, but they were happy cooking at the highest level. They didn't look stressed.

I had never been in a kitchen where everyone was happy. It was so cutthroat in the states, with so much competition. I had experienced it earlier at Vendetta's; I knew Christian wanted my job. Luckily, yet unknown to Christian, I was preparing to give it to him.

Denmark is one of the happiest countries in the world, not because of the country. The country is cold and dark, most of the year, so it's obviously not the country. Everyone seemed to have different values. The best restaurants are the best because they embrace their surroundings and cook with passion. I wanted to cook with the same passion. More importantly, I wanted to be happy.

The chef escorted me to the back of the kitchen. There sat a long table, and in the center of the table stood Chef Kofoed's three Bocuse d'Or awards. I was close enough to touch them, and I damn sure did. I petted the sculptures as if they were my own. Now I had wished I had my camera with me. After I sat at the long table, the chef delivered the signature dish: a razor clam with an edible shell. The chef then explained to me how the shell was a thin cracker that had been painstakingly dyed with squid ink and shaped to resemble the clam's natural shell. A dish with simple ingredients, showing creative techniques. While seated enjoying my simple snack, I even got a glimpse of the man, Rasmus Kofoed himself, in the kitchen wearing an apron. The way a chef should be, slaving away with the rest of the cooks.

Shortly after I returned to my table and had a few more courses, a new guest was invited into the kitchen. It was another single diner. This time, I watched as the chefs gathered around and took a photo with the lucky guest. I sat at my table awaiting my next course. It was my main course of grilled lamb with pickled strawberries. I watched as the chefs took a photo break, curious if the break would affect the flow of service. It did not. My full meal was exactly three hours, as scheduled. I was impressed! In the end, I was served a total of twenty-three courses, all perfectly timed.

The meal as a whole, however, was not perfect. My standards for Michelin-star restaurants may have been a little unrealistic. But, I had traveled across the ocean; thousands of dollars later, I expected absolute perfection. Although the meal was not impeccable, I had decided my timing was. The most inspirational time to visit a restaurant, as a chef, is when the restaurant is still chasing perfection. At two Michelin stars, it was chasing its third. I wondered if they had already achieved that status, would Chef Rasmus have been in that kitchen with an apron? I could still feel the energy and excitement in that kitchen.

As I left the restaurant, I felt quite comfortable. Geranium serves light dishes, a lot of seafood and vegetables. Even after twenty-three courses, I was not full, but I was perfectly satisfied. It was still early in the afternoon, so I decided to explore the city as planned. I had no actual plans to visit any other landmarks, although I would not have minded if I were to stumble across the restaurant Noma. It had a mystique about it as the "best restaurant in the world," but I suspected I was more pleased with Geranium than I would have been at Noma. Having not eaten at Noma, I couldn't judge for certain. But I was glad that Noma had been closed.

While Noma was a foraging restaurant and more rustic, I loved refinement—and I had found it at Geranium. Noma was better known for being experimental, with servings that even included ants. The restaurant had diners cook their own eggs on a table-top burner with instructions. Not my style. By now, I knew exactly what I was looking for in a restaurant. I loved contemporary fine dining. I was extremely inspired by Geranium, and because of that inspiration, the meal was worth every penny, the cost of my flight across the Atlantic included.

By the time I finished exploring the city, it was around ten o'clock at night. I had spent the entire day in Denmark. I decided it was time for me to head back to Helsingborg. I wasn't too comfortable finding my way back to Sweden if it got much later. This time, I opted to take the train rather than the ferry, as it was a much quicker route. After arriving back in Helsingborg, I discovered that The Hippie had borrowed a car to visit a friend up north. She would be gone for a couple days, as it was her only chance to see her friend. The Hippie's dad gave me the news, and since he had just met me, he seemed concerned about me alone in a foriegn land. I wasn't concerned. I was quite capable of entertaining myself.

As I wandered through the historic town, I went out to eat at restaurants. When given a menu written in Swedish, I quickly became aware of how difficult this might be to order my meals. The language was different, but the numbers were the same, so I figured I'd just order the middle-priced items. How could I go wrong?

My strategy worked to perfection, although I'll never know what dishes I might have missed out on. Besides the food and local drinks, I found extreme pleasure in walking along the boardwalk along the North Harbor. Relaxing on the beach, I felt jealous that The Hippie had grown up in a beach town. Then I took a plunge into the frigid water. That's when I realized how far north Sweden is. That water was cold!

Three days had now passed, and I was ready to be reunited with my friend. The Hippie had borrowed her mom's car, so we explored the Swedish countryside, visiting towns like Viking, where I saw the most stereotypical Swedish girls I could have ever imagined: two young girls, probably in their teens, with blue eyes, long blond hair in pigtails, wearing overalls. In addition to visiting Viking, we went to one of The Hippie's favorite restaurants. Located in a small farmhouse, we stopped in for another rather amazing lunch. There is something that must be said about simple food in the countryside. In this family-run restaurant, the meal felt personal and intimate.

While driving around the countryside, we saw many lakes and large fields. I began to realize how much Sweden reminded me of northern Minnesota. After returning to Helsingborg, we helped The Hippie's mom prepare food for the informal reception she was hosting at the house where we were staying at. This is when I realized The Hippie's mom was the biggest "foodie" with the most expensive taste I had ever met. For the reception, they were serving duck with armagnac and confit goose, smoked salmon, and pounds of foie gras. Yes, pounds of the stuff. All to be washed down with bottles of French champagne.

The Hippie also insisted that we must have a kräftskiva, a Swedish crawfish boil. So we went to the market and bought a few pounds of crawfish. It was similar to a New Orleans crawfish boil, with the main exception the aromatic use of dill rather than the use of spices typical of the American south. After inviting her sister to join us, we set up a table with tons of napkins on the cute, little outdoor patio. We popped a bottle of champagne, sucked down the bucket of crustaceans, and the three of us enjoyed the serenity of the cool Swedish night.

The next day was the informal reception. It was a great gathering of people with amazing food. The Hippie's brother was living in New York, where he had met his fiancé, so there were plenty of other Americans there. As usual, there was an awkwardness between the two cultures, so the Americans had a tendency to stick together. I was bonding with them pretty well, but I got antsy and had to hit the town. I left the reception early to find a local pub.

The wedding was the following day. I carpooled with the other Americans to a castle high up in the hills of Helsingborg. The wedding was in a beautiful, old castle with amazing views and a historic atmosphere. I heard the chef catering the special occasion had his own Michelin star credentials. Whether he did or didn't, the food was easily worthy of a star. He served variations of asparagus with dill mousse, a roasted moose loin with green juniper jus, and for dessert a lemon bavarois with rhubarb and hibiscus. I could tell the chef was classically trained in French food. Each dish showcased the ingredients in different forms. For example, for dessert, the hibiscus was served not only as infusion in the cold, marinated rhubarb, but also dehydrated in a fruit leather, and if that wasn't enough, the entire dish was complemented by a hibiscus sorbet. The chef clearly wanted to display his own technique and style. Although not displaying the intricate details of Geranium, the food served at this wedding in a castle in Sweden could certainly rival the quality of the two-Michelin-starred restaurant.

After the wedding, we went out, all dressed up. We headed to the bars of Helsingborg. Dancing in the clubs, I remember attempting to work my magic with the local girls. This would be my only attempt at working any game during the entire trip—and I failed miserably. To this day, I still have no idea what one girl said; she screamed something at me in Swedish. I freaked and realized the effort wasn't worth it. The Swedes clearly weren't as in love with American boys as girls were in the Philippines.

The next day, we planned to head to Switzerland. Back at the house, it was time to repack. The rest of our flights would be on small planes, and I didn't want to check my bag the rest of the way. Instead, I elected to take a small carry-on, leaving my large bag at the house in Sweden. The next day we were back on the train to Copenhagen.

We flew into Geneva, Switzerland, arriving late at night. Although we had carefully planned each of our flights, we had planned the flights with a budget in mind. We had found the most affordable flights, and the timing was not perfect. Arriving at the train station, we discovered we missed the last train to our condo in the mountains of Le Châble in Verbier Valley. We decided to put our bags in lockers at the train station so we would not have to carry them around town. We decided to go explore, looking for a bar and maybe even a possible all-night club.

When we left the confines of the train station, the skies opened up and the rain came pouring down. We found shelter in a nearby parking garage and got chased out by a screaming security guard. With no clue what he was saying, we ran out into the cold rain. We found a nice, little pub and went in for a drink. I asked the lady behind the bar if she spoke English. She shook her hand to indicate a little. We were clearly immersed in the French-speaking land. I asked for a beer, and she just poured me one. I liked that, not like in the states where bartenders give you the big, pretentious spiel. When I want a beer, I just want a refreshing beer—I hated the whole craft beer scene. I'd prefer to walk up to a bar in the states, ask for a beer, and the bartender would simply hand me one. I love simplicity.

The bar closed at two in the morning, standard bar closing in the states. Our bartender directed us to an all-night club. However, after walking in the rain unable to find the club, we were soaked. We decided to head back to the station, retrieve our bags, and hopefully dry up or maybe even change out of our wet clothes.

But back at the station, we discovered we had been locked out. We peeked through the doors, so close to our bags and a little warmth. We were freezing at this point. We decided to wander back out onto the streets to find shelter, and passing by a nearby McDonald's with a canopy over the door, we found the closest thing to shelter. I was curious to see if the famous John

Travolta line from *Pulp Fiction* was true: "Do you know what they call a Big Mac in Switzerland? A Royale with Cheese." They did. Watching the streets, we didn't see any taxis or other transportation options. The city seemed deserted, almost creepy.

After a few minutes outside McDonald's, we decided to search for better shelter. Staying near the station so as not to venture off too far, we found an open area underneath the train station building. This was where we realized we were not alone. Twenty or thirty others had missed their trains and were stranded, too. Freezing from the rain, I decided to remove my drenched hoodie and use it as a pillow in a failed attempt to sleep on the cold tiles. Curled up on the floor, The Hippie and I noticed others trying to sleep standing up. What were they trying to accomplish? Were they afraid if they fell asleep, they would get robbed? We were awake and cold, but at least on the cold tiles our bodies were resting.

Around five in the morning, the station opened and we finally retrieved our bags. We then purchased tickets and caught the first train heading up the mountains. On the two-hour long train up to Le Châble, we headed through low-lying clouds and the rain continued to come down. Visibility was limited, but the clouds only added to the experience. They gave the Swiss Alps a mysterious and mystical feeling, which helped build suspense for when the skies cleared. Plus, being in the clouds made us feel even higher up than we already were.

While booking our trip, Switzerland had been low on my list of priorities. I figured there wasn't much difference between one mountain town to the next. I was completely wrong. I had always heard that mountains in Europe seem bigger, and that was true. They felt monstrous, straight up with sharp peaks. It's not like the Colorado Rockies are mellow or small, but these looked different.

When we finally arrived at the cute, little town of Le Châble at the base of Verbier, we only had a short walk to our condo. After inserting the key into the elevator, we gave it a turn and pushed the button for the top floor. I then learned that The Hippie's parents not only had a good taste in food, but just good taste, in general. We had the top-floor penthouse, with high, vaulted ceilings and a large, private deck extending across the entire top floor. The amazing, well-designed kitchen looked as though it was straight out of an Ikea catalog. I was in love with this condo. I was in love with the mountains of Switzerland.

Our first day, we hiked around the small mountain town, listening to cows mooing in the distance and hearing the bells around their necks banging. From a distance, it was a pleasant reminder of where I was: very far from home. But as the sounds got louder, fear began to sink in. Were we about to get trampled? Farm animals were truly free-ranging in the Alps, not nearly as fenced-in as in the states. Slightly nervous, we changed our course. Back in town, there were few restaurants, much less than most of the cities I'd visited. We did, however, find a nice Italian place, unspectacular but still quite satisfying.

The next day after grabbing a few pastries for breakfast, we took the tiny gondola ride up to Verbier. This was when I realized more major differences between Europe and the states. First of all, that outdated gondola would have been replaced years ago. Secondly, the Swiss Alps were absolutely huge, going straight up. After hiking around for a while, we grabbed some beer so we could really take in the scenery; I was loving it. After building up a good appetite, we decided to get lunch. We were truly dining in the clouds. Sitting on the large, bustling patio with visibility at an absolute minimum, we enjoyed fondue with mountain herbs and a dish of well-prepared risotto with scallops.

After descending the thousands of feet back down to our condo, I decided I wanted to take advantage of that beautiful kitchen, so we went to the market and bought some local meats to grill up. I also felt the need to try the Swiss air-dried meats, all made from local cows. I was hooked with a vision: Why couldn't we do locally air-dried meats like these in Vail? We had the same climate.

Since Switzerland had been low on my priority list and we missed a night stranded in Geneva, we only stayed two days. I wished we could take advantage of that beautiful condo longer. Oh well. It was off to Croatia next. The train ride down to Gene-va seemed longer than the ride up, as I was going to miss Le Châble, but I was excited for my next destination.

After arriving in Split, Croatia, we needed to catch a bus to the port, where the ferry would take us to the island of Hvar. Before leaving the mainland, I noticed a large farmers' market, and I felt the need to see the local produce. As expected, every-thing seemed much fresher than what was possible to grow in the Rocky Mountains. After the quick walk-through, it was onto the ferry. We had been informed that we were unable to stay at The Hippie's parents' beach house because it was under con-struction. So her dad arranged for The Hippie to stay at a friend's house, while renting me a room on another property. I wasn't dating The Hippie, but even if I was, it was not a part of their culture for us to share a room together. I was perfectly fine with having my own place.

We stayed on the less-touristy side of the island in the town of Jelsa, which I was also pleased with. The family hosting The Hippie was welcoming; they invited us to family dinner and showed us the island. They also had their own garden and loved fresh vegetables, including growing their own grapes to make their own wine. I later learned everyone on the island made their own wine. Including restaurants, where house wine was truly house wine—and cheaper than beer.

The family also had a son a little younger than us, but still relatively close to our age. Kind of a crazy driver though. He decided to pick up one of his friends and take us to an area on the island that they called The Top. Careening through the narrow streets and alleys, I was surprised we didn't take anyone out or lose any appendages.

There was a mountain on Hvar island, and at the top was a nice, little resort that his parents owned. It was a popular vacation spot, usually booked all summer long. But we were lucky. The resort was ours for the day. After stopping by a liquor store, we headed up the mountain. We were on our way to poach the most sought-after getaway on the island.

Upon reaching the summit, we understood why it had been promised to be the most popular resort on the island. It was totally secluded with amazing views, similar to a cabin in the mountains, only made of stone rather than wood. The skies were clear, so we could see all the way to Italy. A small building stood with a doorway so small you had to nearly be on your knees to enter. Inside, however, was a room much larger than the exterior suggested. It was still small, but a bed fit inside, along with a rustic-looking, wood-burning stove. On the property, tennis courts and the perfectly constructed infinity pool sat. The pool was the epitome of perfection. With the amazing views, we went for a swim and spent our entire day there.

Once the sun went down, we decided to go back to a friend's place and play cards. Sitting around a table just getting drunk made me feel antsy. Sitting still was not for me. I had to leave. It felt like a high-school party all over again. The Hippie stayed with the guys in the house; I think she felt it would be rude to leave them. I couldn't do it, though. I wanted to see the bar scene. It was a quiet night. I now understood why most of the locals had stayed in. But I did have a couple beers on a nice outside patio.

The next day, The Hippie, the son, and I did what I wanted to do most: relax on the beach. I had heard Croatia was known for some of the best beaches in the world. The rumors were right: They were amazingly beautiful, but I was disappointed to learn they were rocky beaches. I wasn't expecting that. I imagined lying on soft white sand like I had witnessed in Boracay. Although the beaches couldn't compete with the sand of Boracay, the crystal clear waters could. As we roamed the shallow waters, The Hippie warned me not to step on round, sharp, prickly creatures. She couldn't think of the name, but I knew instantly: sea urchins. And through the clear waters, I actually spotted one. I knew from my culinary research that the roe was a delicacy. So I grabbed the spiky creature. It was, however, too small to contain any roe. So I just held onto the shell as a souvenir. The Hippie spotted a sea cucumber, another exotic ingredient I had heard of but never held. So she dove down about ten feet to scoop it up. I really just wanted to inspect the sea vegetable. I had no idea what to do with it, though.

After the sun went down, the peacefulness of the island became ever so apparent. Although it was mid-July, it felt like off-season. I like simply walking around, enjoying the silhouettes of the many boats in the tiny harbor and the small ice cream stands serving exotic-sounding flavors. I had always been a night person, and I realized this was why. I love serenity. Nights are more peaceful.

The next day, we explored more: the city of Hvar, the busy side of the island. Once there, it felt like the temperature went up another twenty degrees. It was fricking hot! A stone jungle, rocks just radiating heat. There were, however, many more restaurants and bars. This time the harbor was not tiny. Massive yachts lined the stretch of waterfront. Yachts so big they even had helicopter-landing pads. Yet a sandy beach once again was not in sight. Instead, beautiful women laid out on the walkway, working on their tans. It was nice to see the touristy side of the island, but I was happy to be staying in Jelsa.

After a couple of drinks, we went for lunch at another one of The Hippie's favorite restaurants from her childhood. She informed me that the restaurant "used to be good," but now since it became popular, the owner was ripping off tourists. The Hippie was adamant about this, so yielding her warning, we only ordered some house wine and an octopus salad. The owner was also the main server in the tiny, family restaurant, so she asked us if the octopus salad was for the three of us. We said it was. The menu had no prices, and after my worldly adventures I had realized this was how many family restaurants operated. They then prepared an octopus salad for three. Overall, the salad was excellent, simply dressed. It was evident that Croatians value their olive oil. I'd experienced this since I'd arrived; they often favor using heavier olive oils with a very pronounced flavor.

However, after the conversion, the salad ended up costing about $50—a rip-off for what we were served. Breaking down the price by three, the price was reasonable—back in the states. But, in Croatia, it was clear we had been taken advantage of. The salad may have been disappointingly expensive, but the house wine and waterfront views were amazing.

There was yet another restaurant that The Hippie proclaimed as an absolute must. We could never leave without trying the best lamb and beef peka on the island. This traditional, slow-cooked dish of meat and vegetables is cooked long, covered and buried under hot coals—cooked for hours. Our hosts agreed it was a must-try during our visit and called in a reservation for all of us.

I was taken away by the decor of the restaurant. It was an open-aired restaurant that appeared as though it had been dug out of the side of a rock—a cave, yet not fully enclosed. We were seated at a booth, dug out deeper into the rock to create a more private table. I had never witnessed a restaurant quite like this one, a magical place. We once again ordered the house wine, as always house-made and served in a carafe. Then our pre-ordered peka arrived, steaming hot and deserving of all the hype.

This was our last night on the island. The Hippie had an early 7 a.m. ferry to catch. I had an extra day to spend however I wanted. The Hippie needed to take care of a few more personal things back in Sweden, and I chose to spend my extra day in a tropical paradise before our flight out of Copenhagen back to the states.

Although I had an extra day, I decided to join The Hippie on that early ferry. I wanted to explore Split on the mainland. Realizing our ferry was early, we decided to try to pull an all-nighter. We walked past a dance club that seemed to be happening, crowded and rocking. After dipping our heads in for a brief moment, we realized the club was a bad idea. Further proof that we were no longer in the states: the club was full of "underage" kids. As the drinking age was much younger, or nonexistent, the club scene was not for us.

We decided to pick up some wine and headed to the nearby park. It felt like I was back in high school, drinking in the park like we were not allowed into the bar. As the night began to drag on, we hit a wall. With the amount of booze we had now consumed, we realized we were not going to make it until our early ferry. Around 4 or 5 a.m., we passed out with ease. I was concerned about missing the ferry, since I was relying on The Hippie. Surely, The Hippie was running on Hippie Time. She was drinking Long Islands all night, after all.

Much to our surprise, we made it on that early ferry. Back in Split, I left The Hippie to catch her bus to the airport and said my goodbyes with plans of seeing her again in Helsingborg. I now needed to find out where I was going to stay. Around the port there were many locals holding signs offering spare bedrooms, or lock-offs, and even someone advertising for a hostel. Before I committed to a place to stay, I decided I should check my bank account. I swiped my card with an attempt to retrieve money. Declined! The two credit cards I owned were both maxed out. I had spent an excessive amount of money in Switzerland; I didn't realize the conversion rate until I was back in the states. Not to mention the cost of high-end, Michelin-starred restaurants. I was virtually broke.

Now a bit of concern set in, but only a little bit. I still had cash in my wallet, so I wasn't too concerned. I had survived an attempt to sleep soaking wet on cold tiles in Switzerland. Surely I was capable of surviving a night outside in warm Croatia. I decided with the cash in my pocket I would be fine to get a room. I would just bargain shop. I began with the hostel. I thought surely it would be the cheapest. I had heard of the stories of college kids backpacking through Europe and sleeping in hostels, so I had to at least check it out. I asked the lady, and she walked me a few blocks toward the downtown area and to a multi-floored apartment. An unimpressive accommodation. I decided to explore other options.

I found another woman offering a lock-off for an inexpensive 350 kunas, less than $50. I explained to her my financial situation and managed to talk her down 50 kunas, which brought the price of the room down to the same price I was offered for the hostel. I walked to her apartment nearby, she opened her lock-off, and I was amazed. It was professionally maintained with a fully made bed, mini fridge, and a clean, private bath. She then gave me directions to her favorite restaurant. I figured I had enough cash to splurge one more time. As I followed her recommendation, I was surprised yet open-minded. Although crowded, it did not appear as though it was a restaurant. Just a group of picnic tables on a patio.

After my negotiation with my new host, I felt obligated to trust her, so I inquired about a seat for one. It was community seating, so I was to enjoy a meal with a bunch of strangers from around the world. And I loved it. Knowing this would be my last meal in a far-away land, I splurged the best my budget would allow. I wanted seafood before heading back to land-locked Colorado, so I ordered the grilled sea bream with buttered rice and salted sardines. As always, I love simplicity. I struck up a friendly conversation with a nearby table mate, and he said he had also recently visited Copenhagen. Although the focus of my trip had largely been on Michelin-star food, our conversation revolved primarily around the people—the friendliest people I have ever met.

After the meal, I did as I had planned. I explored the city of Split. As my funds had dwindled, I found myself just walking along the waterfront, lined with many enormous yachts like I had seen earlier in Hvar. In the center of the port, a crowd gathered, so I went over to investigate. They were watching a street performance. During the introductions, they also explained where the performers were from. I was surprised to learn that the performers were from all over the world, including the United States. The performance was similar to a dance off, with a lot of break dancing moves that seemed well choreographed. After the show, I explored more of the port area; after seeing the downtown area where the hostel was located, I had no interest in heading back in that direction. Seaside seemed like the nicer part of town. I passed more restaurants and street food vendors. The Hippie had told me I should try the ćevapčići, meaning "little fingers," a sausage sandwich, so I did.

When morning came, I was back on a flight back to Copenhagen. I knew I had told The Hippie I would meet her in Helsingborg, but I simply couldn't. Without a working credit card, I was stranded in the airport for the night. With no cell phone, I couldn't inform The Hippie of my situation. She was my backup plan if I ran out of funds on this trip. I had to leave my bags in Sweden until god knows when (it ended up taking four years to get them back), and I just hung out hungry in the airport, unable to sleep, until The Hippie arrived and our flight finally departed. I decided to suck it up, since I was preparing to start a new life after Vendetta's in Vail when I got home anyway.

A Kräftskiva in Sweden

In the mountains of Le Chablis, Switzerland

Eating ćevapčići on the streets of Split, Croatia

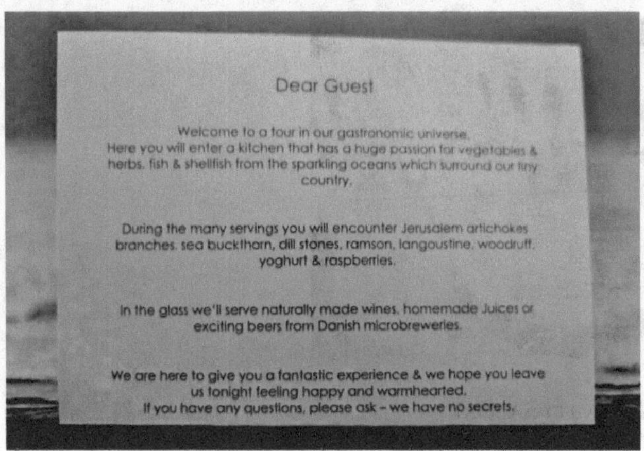



My welcome note at Geranium, "they have no secrets"

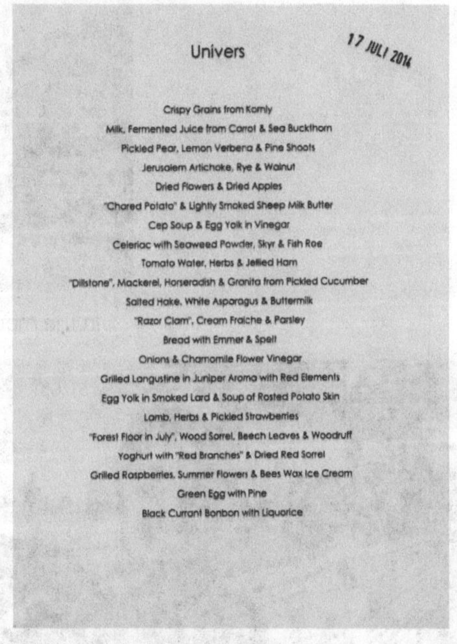



Geranium's menu containing 22 of the
23 dishes I was served

# Chapter 12:

## The Smallest Kitchen in the World

I returned to Vail, fully recharged and energized. Geranium had shown me dining at another level. I wanted my Vail family to know what it was like to enjoy a life-changing meal, just like I'd had in Copenhagen. I wanted to transform the way we dined in Vail. I wanted to put Vail on the global culinary map. I wanted to cook with the same passion I'd witnessed throughout Europe. I saw happy people in kitchens, something I'd rarely seen in the states. I questioned why kitchens were so much more ego-driven here. Why couldn't Americans treat everyone equal, regardless of social hierarchy? I wondered why our values were so fucked.

Life seemed better in Europe. I was so inspired by Europe and travel that I was eager to see more. I had caught the travel bug, and becoming more cultured was my new dream. I had no idea how I was going to pull it off, but I'd found a dream worth chasing after. I remembered Danny had spent two years working in Europe. I thought about following in his footsteps.

But even after traveling to some of the most amazing places in Europe, I knew Vail was definitely home to me. After living there for almost fifteen years, there was no other place in the world I would rather live. However, I was well aware of the difficult housing issues that plagued ski towns. Although I had an apartment that I had been renting for a few years now, I needed something more permanent.

I sent my brother a text. He had been a CEO at Ameriprise Financial for twenty years now, and I knew he was financially well-off. In my text, I suggested that he buy a condo in Vail, so at least my rent money would stay in the family. I asked him exactly like that; I didn't want it to sound like I was looking for a freebie, and didn't mention to him my thoughts about some day to leaving town. I figured if I left, I could easily rent out the apartment. I just wanted to know when I returned, I would have a place to stay.

My brother instantly gave me a call, eager to help me out. My next priority was that I needed a job, so I needed to write a resume. Although I had worked many part-time and side jobs over the past ten years while at Vendetta's, I'd never really needed a resume. Most of my jobs up until this point I had gotten through friend recommendations, so this was completely new to me. I researched sample resumes on the internet and managed to write up something that at least resembled some sort of professionalism. Times had changed since I had last been on a true job search, and most people simply applied over the internet. But I decided to do it old-school style: Make it personal and deliver my resume by hand. There was really only one restaurant in town that I had my eyes set on. Although I was confident, if my strategy didn't work, I had no other backup plan.

Knowing my love for European-style dining, I figured La Tour was my only logical choice. La Tour had long been a Vail institution, known for turning out one great chef after another. Although, lately the restaurant had come across some hard times, which had become apparent by the brown disposable paper being used as table cloths. No longer able to afford the sky-rocketing cleaning costs of white linens, the paper was a more viable option. Behind the great success of La Tour was the husband-wife team of Lourdes and chef Paul Ferzacca. After more than fifteen years running the restaurant, it was understandable and becoming visibly obvious they were burning out.

In the late nineties and early 2000s, Chef Paul made headlines, won awards, made guest appearances, and earned James Beard honors. I may be a little biased being from Vail, but after Chef Paul mentored the local high school ProStart team to numerous state wins and even a national championship, I considered him to be one of the best chefs in the entire country. So with my resume in hand, I walked into La Tour and asked the first person I saw to speak to the chef or kitchen manager. She returned with the executive chef, Troy. He, however, had already turned in his notice. Troy's wife was pregnant, and he was about to start a family. He directed me to the chef de cuisine, Joe.

We took a seat at a table in the back of the restaurant and had a quick chat. I don't know whether Joe even looked at my resume, but regardless, I was invited back the next week for a stage. A stage is simply a tryout. Most up-and-coming cooks fear a stage as a test to see what they are capable of. A stage, however, goes both ways. I also wanted to know if the restaurant was right for me.

I arrived for my stage the following week. I was placed on the fish station and primarily I just observed. After the stage, I was invited to sit down at the bar and order a free meal. Following my love of fish and simplicity, I ordered the Dover sole classically served with potatoes and brown butter. My real knowledge of this type of dining was still limited. I was ignorant and unaware of the price of true imported Dover sole. Joe replied with "Just going all out, huh?" I had, in fact, ordered the most expensive entree on the menu.

Joe, however, wasn't too concerned with the cost. He even sent out a few more appetizers for me to try, resulting in a three- or four-course meal. As I was eating, Joe sat down and asked me what I thought. I said I felt I would be a good addition to his team. Having friends who had worked there before, I knew how much La Tour was willing to pay. So, taking a good-sized pay cut from my previous position, I was offered the modest hourly wage I had asked for.

La Tour was an extremely challenging kitchen, and I'm not just talking about maintaining the high standards. La Tour had a tiny kitchen, about three hundred square feet, with an old tile floor and tiled walls. It hadn't received any sort of upgrades over the last two decades, so the equipment was outdated and on its last legs. The walk-in freezer and fridge were both located out the back door, down a set of stairs outside, and in the open-air parking garage—often with wind and snow drifting through. The main prep room and dry storage area were located even farther away. Our prep room, only a third the size of our kitchen, contained nothing more than a large stainless steel table and a three-compartment sink for doing dishes. We had no way of actually doing any cooking—just knife work. Massive pots of stocks and sauces were made upstairs, and once finished, carried down the stairs to be iced down in the prep room sinks. The stairs created a major physical challenge, and I knew they were going to be hell. Regardless, nothing mattered. I loved the challenges and I needed money, so I was ready to work.

I had watched old videos of British chef Marco Pierre White

at work at Harveys; La Tour's outdated kitchen closely resembled the one in which Marco had become famous. It seriously looked like the kitchen had never left the eighties. When I first began work at La Tour, I once again suffered from insomnia—the same insomnia I had experienced a few years earlier when I had left Vendetta's to join Scooby at The Lord Gore. A crazy vertigo feeling. Only this time, the sensation was even crazier, or at least my actions were a lot crazier. I didn't sleep for several days. Honestly, I didn't know how many days it had been. With insomnia, time feels like one really long day, because it is; your body needs sleep to tell the difference. The insomnia had affected me so badly that I got to the point where I was unable to decipher between what was reality or what was a dream.

I was sitting at home, possibly even lying in bed. I'm not sure, but I felt like I was supposed to be at work. So, I walked into La Tour screaming that I was the executive chef, or maybe I was asking if I was the executive chef. Possibly both. I was confused and fighting with my brain to realize what was reality and what wasn't. My weakened mental state had me believing I was, in fact, Marco Pierre White. Although I couldn't think clearly, I must have at least had enough trust in my new teammates, because they managed to convince me I needed to go home. One of the line cooks, Jordan, was particularly concerned over my safety and told me it wasn't safe for me to be out on the streets.

The event was not the type of first impression I would have liked to have given my new teammates. But I had no control over my actions. I had scared my new team severely. Everyone from Chef Paul downward thought I was on drugs. The insomnia continued throughout my first few weeks of work. My coworkers had to constantly remind me what was real. I truly believed I was

Marco Pierre White, and not just Marco Pierre White, but Marco Pierre White in the eighties. Some of my coworkers laughed at me, as I understand on the outside it could have been funny. It was embarrassing, but it was actually a serious situation. I was struggling to fight a mental illness. Anxiety wouldn't let my brain rest. I could have easily been pushed the wrong way, landing me in a mental hospital.

While I was struggling to get settled into my new job, I still was dealing with stress outside of work: finding a home. To help with the search, I needed a realtor. I posted on social media to see if I had any friends or friends of friends. After a good amount of responses, I settled on Chris. His brother, Mark, was of large stature, and I knew Mark from his days of working the door at Vendetta's. Vendetta's was open late at night, so we often had to deal with uncooperative drunks. I figured Mark's brother working with my brother would be quite fitting. So, with Chris's assistance, we began searching for one- or two-bedroom condos. As I expected, there weren't many options. However, Chris was extremely helpful. At all hours of the day and night, Chris sent me texts the moment a condo hit the market. It would be midnight, and I would get a text. The first thing in the morning, Chris would pick me up to check the place out.

I'd lost my driver's license years earlier, due to an unpaid minor traffic ticket. I paid it, only late. The state had sent me a letter, but I never received it, probably because I moved around a lot in my earlier years. So the state suspended my license for a year. No license for a year meant I had to take the test over, but I never bothered. Gas prices had skyrocketed, and I couldn't afford a car anyway. I figured life would be simpler without one.

The search for an apartment started to feel impossible. Although we had looked at quite a few, my brother was being picky. It was his money, after all, and I knew he wanted to find the perfect situation for both of us. I was beginning to feel annoyed and done with the stress. I was ready to give up. I wanted my main focus to be on La Tour.

My brother sent me a spreadsheet. I didn't even know where the numbers had come from, but I reviewed them. I was done with the stress and texted back that I didn't think I could afford a place. But he didn't let me give up. We finally settled on a two-bedroom, just down the street from where I was living. I was familiar with the neighborhood. It was the perfect location close to work. I knew I would be working crazy hours, often late at night after the last buses departed. Not owning a car or driver's license, I needed something within walking distance.

The condo appeared like the previous owners had begun remodeling—then gave up. The kitchen had new appliances, but was poorly designed and could use new cabinets. The fireplace was made with beautiful stone and appeared brand new, while upstairs, the carpet—although more modern than the shag of the sixties and seventies—could have used upgrading. The doors were recently replaced. The door of the master bedroom wasn't properly fitted with the jam. The door knobs were new: Baldwin, of the highest quality. The walk-in closet's door knob was missing. But, what needed the most upgrading was the disgustingly ugly vanity in the bathroom. It looked like an old dresser from the seventies, made of wood with decorative molding as though it was carved by hand. I liked a more mass-produced look. Simple.

Then came the furniture. The place had come fully furnished, but more accurately, it just wasn't fully cleaned out. There was straight junk in the closet, and the furniture was old and gross.

Beyond outdated, it was classic grandma-style furniture. It had to go. I decided to get rid of everything except for the beds.

With my new condo empty, I could start from scratch. I had never furnished my own apartment before. I always settled for whatever furniture the apartment came with. Financially certain luxuries were never a priority. But now I had my own place. I was excited.

My sister-in-law, Amy, flew out to Colorado to help me furnish my new place. I had no sense of style or decor, so everything was new to me. At the condo, Amy did a quick scan to see what we were working with. She asked what colors I liked. I said black and white, a modern look. We headed to Denver. American Furniture Warehouse and Ikea were our choices, and Amy made the shopping as painless as possible. After setting up my new furniture for delivery, I headed back to Vail.

My next objective was to find a roommate, and honestly, I wasn't trying to be too picky. Over the years, I had lived with all kinds of crazies. In fact, there was a chance I might have been the craziest of them all. I was just looking for someone responsible enough to pay the rent. I was well aware of the fact that I would never be home; forget about the job and the hours I would put in there, I just didn't like to sit still. I was never much of a homebody.

My first roommate failed, unable to fulfill my only two requirements: being responsible and paying the rent. I settled on my longtime friend, Jay, although he more commonly went by his last name, Krause. Krause was a local, having moved to Vail a year before I did. Krause had a steady job—the same job for as long as I had known him. I had no doubt that Krause would be reliable. He was the perfect roommate. Krause was a homebody who would take care of my new condo better than I ever could.

Now with my living situation all settled, I could finally focus on my new job. Although I was no longer an employee of Vendetta's, it still felt like home to me. I went into Vendetta's one evening, and it felt slightly awkward. Some of the staff members were happy for me because I was moving on, but I could feel a little resentment from others; they thought I had left because I felt I was better than them. Regardless of the discomfort, I sat down at the pizza bar and was handed a beer. As I finished my beer, another beer arrived. It was from my new boss, Chef Paul.

Paul and Lourdes were sitting directly across from me. I hadn't noticed them. I went over for a chat and thanked them for my beer. Chef Paul responded with a simple, "Thank you." I was just a line cook at the time, but no other explanation was needed. Chef Paul had been waiting for someone like me to walk through his door. He knew, because I had just done the exact same thing he had done upon opening La Tour: He had traveled through Europe and been inspired. Although the food in Europe had been amazing, the happy feeling in the kitchen at Geranium kept replaying in my mind.

During my first winter at La Tour, Chef Paul was still working the pass almost every night. While I was on the line, I loved when he worked the pass. His standards were exactly how they should be, and he liked to yell. I absolutely loved that about him. I remember one time there was food up, and I quietly and calmly mentioned to him that it needed to get run. He looked at me and said, "You can yell at me, too, ya know." From that moment, I had no problem yelling at him when food needed to get run. Our guests always came first. He knew it and I knew it. And we both knew being yelled at was never personal.

Then one day, our grill cook was struggling. He asked me how we did it at Vendetta's, because he knew how busy that restaurant got—and cooking steaks is cooking steaks.

"We didn't have the same staff turnover you have here," I said. He wondered why, but I didn't have an answer. "I like it here, so I can't tell you."

In fact, I did like it there. I wanted to be a part of the stress, the pressure, and everyone needed to have thick skin. Chef Paul telling me I could yell at him, too, was exactly what I wanted to hear. It meant equal treatment for everyone, regardless of who they were.

One day during closing time, I was cleaning my station and looked across at expo and noticed the soups weren't being iced down. Soup usually takes more than an hour to cool to a safe temperature for storage. So I went over and got Chef Paul's soup on ice. When he returned to the kitchen, he noticed the soup was icing down for him already.

"Who did this?" he asked.

I answered. "I did, chef, none of us want to be here all night."

He responded with "Yeah, and I got here at ten! Not two." That was the time his sous chefs clocked in.

Chef Paul was pretty much opening and closing. Everyone else expected him to do that because he owned the place and was obligated to. When it was Chef Paul and me closing, we were often there until nearly two in the morning. Excessive cleaning was usually needed with him around.

From the second I got there, it was apparent I was more dedicated than most cooks he had seen. It was clear I was not your ordinary, run-of-the-mill line cook. I was already showing leadership skills.

We had a young, inexperienced cook, Manny, working pantry trying to make crackers. He didn't really know what he was doing, so I went over to help him. After making the dough, it was then rolled out using a pasta roller. I asked the sous chef what number the roller should be set at. He didn't have an answer, so I told the cook, "Well, let's just see what your other crackers look like." When I showed him how simple it was, he was the happiest kid in the world. He wanted to learn. I knew it! The drive in this industry is all about personal development and growth. Often that growth doesn't just mean culinary skills.

I had gone through tremendous personal growth during my time at Vendetta's. At first, I was extremely timid and lacked confidence. I knew now that building these young kids' confidence was paramount. I was driven by what I had seen in the Geranium kitchen, how happy everybody was. I just imagined how much better the food could be if the people making it were actually happy.

I thought back on how I had started at Vendetta's, how Danny was the only one I felt I could approach. Joe and Aaron, in particular, were intimidating. My development was slow, because I was scared. I was a young kid with no experience, but wanted to learn. I was exactly like Manny. He wanted to learn, and I was now in a position where I could help him. Crackers are one of the easiest things to make. Flour, water, and salt rolled thin and baked. There you have a cracker. Yet he needed help. I wanted to let him know not to be scared to ask anything. I didn't want him to feel intimidated. I wanted to set an example that this job wasn't that hard.

I was talking to one of our servers, Lauren. Lauren had been La Tour's longest-running staff member, close to ten years. Lauren also just happened to be my longtime skater buddy Jay's girlfriend. Jay was actually the one who had started all the skate trips we took during my early years at Vendetta's. He always raved to her about those skate trips, and I told her I had been on those trips with Jay. I told her about one of the skate parks in Portland, the legendary Burnside Park.

Burnside was a bridge in Portland under which the homeless and heroin addicts hung out, and it was greatly neglected by the city. Then sometime in the nineties, a group of skaters started pouring concrete. With no permission from the city, they started building their own skate park. The skaters built a renegade park, and I proclaimed to Lauren how it had since been signed off to the city, making it an official city park. I told her how it had been built by guys like me, and that was why the skate park was so rough and challenging. It was because the guys had no idea how to pour concrete, they just wanted to build something to skate. Burnside's defining character is that it's a tough place to skate; it wasn't challenging on purpose.

I went on to talk about how I had helped build Vail's original skate park. Even though she never skated, Lauren knew about how much better flow that park had than the recently professionally built park. I told her that it was because we built it, and if we didn't like something about it, we did something about it. I explained how the halfpipe was too big for most of our skill levels, so the next year we made it shorter. We had grown with that park. As we got better, so did the park. The park had better flow because we were the ones who skated it every day, often rearranging the ramps or building additional features the following year. If we wanted to make it better, it was our responsibility, which also included acquiring the funds.

Lauren understood my point. If we wanted La Tour to get better, it was our responsibility.

Although Chef Paul and Lourdes owned the place, it didn't matter. I wanted La Tour to get better, so it was up to me to make it better. I also raved to Lauren about my experience traveling through Europe and my passion for food, my experiences dining at Michelin-starred restaurants, meeting the chefs. I told her about my train ride up the Swiss Alps and how majestic it was, asking if she ever rode a train in the Swiss Alps. I spoke with extreme enthusiasm and passion. Lauren had been at La Tour longer than anyone except the owners, but I had brought renewed life and energy to the restaurant, and she wasn't the only one who was taking notice.

One night after work, I was hanging out at The George with many of our front of house staff. "Bamma," who had been at La Tour for a long time as well, was sitting next to me. He was excited about the kitchen staff and raved about how much talent and knowledge was now in that kitchen, bringing up our sous chefs Preston and Jordan. Jordan was our newest, brought over after years at Sweet Basil. Bamma was excited about how much they knew. He continued on about how excited he was about me, how much I knew.

I told him with enthusiasm, "We're about to blow the fuck up. I guarantee it. We're gonna do three hundred covers a night. Smallest kitchen in the world, and we're gonna make this shit look easy."

I had a clear emphasis on the word "look." I wanted to change the perception that cooking at a high level was challenging. I wanted to make the whining crybabies shut up and recreate the industry's image. A negative attitude hurts the industry and is contagious, and I was over being surrounded by it. I had made a huge scene at The George with my enthusiasm and everyone had taken notice. During my time at Vendetta's, I witnessed a major remodel and then an even bigger expansion. I knew what it would take, but having already experienced it once, I now had the confidence I could do it again. I wanted to prove I was up to the challenge to restore La Tour's glory.

Although I respected our sous chefs, I began questioning their leadership skills. I thought about Manny and his simple cracker dilemma. When I had just started working there, and I looked to a sous chef for help, but I didn't get any. I needed my own solution. The cooks were even doing their own prep sheets. I wondered what the sous chefs actually did.

I was filling out my prep sheet one night and realized there was a lot to do, so I asked Chef Paul if he minded if I came in a little earlier. He looked at Preston, waiting for a response, but Preston remained silent. Chef Paul was looking for someone to lead his kitchen, and he wasn't finding it in his sous chefs.

Chef Paul told me to come in at two, an hour early. He reiterated it back to Preston: "He's coming in at two."

I could feel Chef Paul's anger. This was the same time the sous chefs were scheduled to start their shift. Preston should have been the one coming in earlier, not me. But I didn't mind. I knew how much work needed to be done. It was irritating, but I did like our sous chefs. I considered them friends; we often went out for drinks together. They just happened to be young and reminded me of myself early in my career.

One day I looked at Preston and said, "You just need to take ownership." He laughed at me, but I was serious. He just didn't know what I meant by "ownership."

*Why wouldn't you actually "own" what you do?* I wondered.

When I began at La Tour, it seemed like everyone feared Chef Paul. I certainly didn't. He definitely was no Popeye. Chef Paul was my size. Popeye was twice my size. Popeye had threatened to "rip my fucking head off," and I believed him when he said that (he had a proven track record). Clearly if we had a real problem I could take Chef Paul. Not Popeye. Vendetta's had turned me into a man. I didn't fear much at this point.

I knew I could never open a restaurant at this level without an investor. Chef Paul was burning out, and I had even heard the restaurant was for sale. He wanted to retire. I knew this, so I considered him more like an investor. Since he was also a chef, I considered him an investor that wouldn't let me fail. I felt I was in the perfect situation. Chef Paul had already invested in me by hiring me, and I was taking ownership of La Tour. I considered myself an owner with a guaranteed paycheck.

My first winter was actually pretty fun. I was, after all, just a line cook with few real responsibilities. I could push those off to the sous chefs. We had a pretty good staff that winter, as well. It was fun; we would go out after work, bonding like a team. We even got Chef Paul to go out to the bars with us. One night he got drunk, too drunk to drive home, so he slept at the restaurant. Lourdes was pretty pissed, mainly because he didn't call to let her know where he was. But Chef Paul wasn't the only one sleeping at the restaurant. My fellow line cook, Colby, would often sleep in our changing room, too. I could also tell Chef Paul was enjoying feeling young again. It was nice seeing him out; I never saw him in bars that much.

We still had yet to find a suitable executive chef, though. At some point that winter Chef Paul contacted one of his old friends, Thomas, a culinary graduate from the prestigious Culinary Institute of America—the CIA. Chef Paul had worked with Thomas in the past, as Thomas had been his executive chef when he opened his other restaurant, ZaccaZa (which has since closed). Factoring in Thomas's experiences, he decided to reunite with his old buddy to be La Tour's new executive chef. Not long after Thomas started, all the other chefs quit, except Joe. Most didn't make it past Christmas.

Nearing springtime, I was working downstairs, alone in the prep room one afternoon, and Chef Thomas casually joined me to strike up a conversation. He asked me how much money I wanted if I was promoted to sous chef. I brought up the fact that I had just bought a condo and told him the lowest yearly salary I was willing to do it for.

"This is as little as I can get by with to pay my bills," I explained. "Right now as a line cook, I still have the time to get a second job." I was well aware of the hours I would need to dedicate to the restaurant if I took on the position.

A few days passed, and Thomas walked up to me and handed me a piece of paper. On the paper had the salary I had requested, in addition to my other benefits, followed by a line for our signatures. I signed on the line, and we shook hands. It was official. I was the new sous chef.

# Chapter 13:

## You Don't Need to Go

During my first training day as sous chef, Thomas walked me around the property pointing to the mess around our Dumpsters. He then told me, pointing at the trash on the ground, "This is where you go tell the dishwasher to go get a broom." The whole time I wondered why we didn't just bring a broom; then it would be done already. But Thomas was now teaching me leadership skills. And the message was becoming clear: I was no longer a line cook.

Toward the end of the shift, I knew we needed to cook some octopus. Octopus takes about four and a half hours to cook. I started it at the end of the night, after service while we were cleaning. The octopus wasn't cooked by the time I was ready to leave, but I pulled it out anyway. I could have just left a note and the opening chef would have taken care of it. However, I still felt the responsibility to ensure it got done. So I came in around eleven the next day. Chef Paul saw me.

"You're here early," he said, surprised. He was clearly used to the sous chefs coming in at two.

Thomas basically trained me on every aspect of my new position, starting with expediting. I had watched Chef Paul train many of the chefs before me, and he had specifics. Very detailed instructions. A full printout even. But during my training, I never saw that printout. Chef Thomas just trained me on the fly, which was fine. I wasn't there alone too often at the beginning. Chef

Paul or Thomas would usually be in the office. I was actually counting on one of them to bail me out if shit was about to hit the fan.

Then one day I was casually perusing the pantry station and saw some poorly cut daikon. Lexi was currently working that station so I asked, "Was this you?" She chuckled, as she knew those knife cuts were a joke, and said no. The actual culprit was the morning cook, who was standing right behind her. He quickly took the blame and stopped what he was doing.

"That was me," he said. "I'll fix it." He proceeded to blame the dull knife he'd used.

"Get a different knife!" I yelled. "Sharpen that shit."

I could see out of the corner of my eye Chef Paul getting some ice. He obviously heard me. Shortly thereafter, he walked through the kitchen and said he wasn't sticking around.

I said, "I'm not too worried. There's only sixty in the books."

He casually replied, "I'm not either." I could tell by the tone of his voice he trusted me. This was the first night I was solely responsible for dinner service.

Chef Thomas was probably the most instrumental to my development—at La Tour, as well as in my life at this point. Any issues I had with the staff, I first brought up to Thomas. He then instructed me that I had to sit down with the staff member for an adult conversation. Previously in my career, emotions would have gotten the best of me. My anger was not controllable. I would often yell at staff members, resulting in frequent walkouts and a high staff turnover. Thomas was now teaching me to deal with situations in a better way.

A few months had passed since I had been promoted, and I talked to Chef Paul about possibly leaving La Tour to work in

Europe. He didn't seem to like the idea. However, he did offer to write me a letter of recommendation if I were to go through with it. Although not really certain of my true intentions, I went home and wrote a long, detailed email to Geranium inquiring about a mere four-to five-day stage.

A week or so later, Chef Paul asked me, "Well?" The one word was following up on my decision to leave for Europe. "You don't need to go," he continued. "You can just stay right here."

He was, in fact, right. I had dreamed of European Michelin-starred kitchens, fantasizing about the aura of them. After experiencing the restaurants firsthand, the aura was gone. My expectation of Michelin-star food had been too high. No longer was Michelin-star food some elusive, mysterious, distant fantasy. What the Michelin chefs did was incredible, but I preferred a different style. They served crackers shaped like branches in a vase with other real branches, and you couldn't tell the difference. I'd found myself chewing on an actual stick. Not sure I could replicate that, nor did I think I wanted to.

I didn't need to go to Europe to work. My letter to Geranium was closure.

When our manager, Abby, left to manage a restaurant in Denver, she dealt with many complaints about the decor of her new restaurant. She wondered why she rarely got complaints about our disgusting carpets at La Tour. Then one day, a guest made a comment that in Vail, people have their "blinders on." The resort of Vail has a magical aura about it. Our guests already have a preconceived fascination of glamour, which blinds them from reality.

This helped me realize I had also been blinded by the magic of European Michelin-star dining. Before, I had never been to

Europe nor experienced that level of dining. I was distracted. Once I took away my blinders, I thought of the food as bland, simplistic, and a low quality for the price I paid. I had paid for the artistry and the experience rather than the actual quality of the food being served. I wanted my focus to remain on the quality—not the illusion.

La Tour had been transforming over recent years to a more casual restaurant, which I assumed was an attempt to adapt with the changes in the industry. So as a way to generate more income, Chef Paul had decided to begin serving lunch as well as dinner. Dinner service had long been the restaurant's focal point, but now the Ferzaccas were changing strategies.

As I was becoming fully dedicated to La Tour, everything began falling into place. Joe was still La Tour's chef de cuisine, but he began filling in the same old role that Rafa had assumed at Vendetta's. Joe would open the restaurant around six in the morning and primarily only work lunch service, often leaving around four. I was beginning to feel a disconnect with Joe, as though he was also preparing to move on from La Tour. I was our only sous chef at the time and had become largely responsible for ensuring a successful dinner service, just as I had done at Vendetta's.

Chef Thomas's role became quite complicated. I'm not sure what Chef Paul had done, but apparently he must have recruited Thomas aggressively. Thomas was married with a small family and living in Denver, a nearly two-hour drive up the mountains to Vail. Thomas would drive up to Vail for the start of his workweek and literally sleep at the restaurant, if he were to sleep at all. One day, I noticed one of his eyes, just one, was completely red. I questioned him about it, and he said he had popped a blood vessel in his eye from it being open too much from constantly being awake. Thomas was surviving off copious amounts of coffee; he needed the caffeine to survive. After a week of quite literally nonstop work, he would then drive back down to Denver for his two days off and be with his family.

I was quite certain Thomas suffered from insomnia, as well. It seemed as though Thomas never stopped thinking about the restaurant—at least not for the entire workweek he lived there. I received emails from him every day, sometimes up to ten or twelve a day. I have never been into checking my email regularly, so many would go unnoticed. But he would send me all kinds of business strategies and new menu ideas. I remember the first menu he sent me to ask my thoughts. It was a lunch menu, and a few changes caught my eye.

First of all, the menu included hamburgers. Our menu had never contained hamburgers before. My only response was I didn't want to serve burgers; I didn't come to La Tour to flip burgers. But I understood the reasoning: Burgers sell. Second, since La Tour didn't own a deep fryer, our sandwiches initially were being served with salads, a potato, and cucumber. The potato and cucumber salads had been replaced by store-bought potato chips. My initial thought was, well, that sounded lazy. However, the concept was actually genius. I had never paid too much attention to our lunch menu up until this point. I only now realized our lunch menu was just there to make the restaurant money, not for showing off our culinary skills.

When Joe and our opening cooks arrived in the morning, they basically set up the line for dinner service. Lunch was nothing more than proteins, usually off our dinner menu, put on either a sandwich or a dinner salad. Not much else. They required little effort for execution or prep, so dinner could be our main focus. Chef Paul and Thomas must have had this figured out. La Tour was only open for lunch, because someone had to be there early to get the prep work started anyway. Our stocks and sauces needed to simmer for six hours or more, so we had a chef come in at six in the morning. We figured we might as well serve a few guests while we were there.

As I was becoming accustomed to the life of a sous chef, Thomas informed me he wanted my priorities to be on butchering our proteins during the morning and early afternoon and expediting dinner service at night. On the days we would work together, Thomas was mainly in the office trying to get our financials in order. As Thomas was scanning through our inventory, he had noticed we were sitting on several pounds of Iberico pork. Iberico pork, being imported from Spain and expensive, was not being served on our menu at the time, so he instructed me to come up with a special.

As I was beginning to brainstorm ideas, one of our inexperienced cooks accidentally made our coconut sauce using almond milk rather than coconut milk. In his defense, the sauce did contain almonds. I tasted the sauce, and it was actually really good, so I decided to use it for my special. Almonds and Iberico ham went great together. So my first special I ran at La Tour was actually the result of someone's fuckup.

My first summer as the sous chef was probably when I developed the most. I knew I still had a lot to learn. I had pretty much everything to learn, as Vendetta's had been my only true, on-the-job training. I needed Thomas. In my opinion, he was a complete chef. Thomas had to show me how to properly butcher both meat and whole fish, as La Tour had its own special way the proteins needed to be portioned. Thomas was a master of these techniques. He was able to break down, pin bone, and portion a whole salmon in just a few minutes. Thomas helped me learn the proper way to position my body so I was efficient. I later learned, from one of my cooks who had also attended the CIA, that he had definitely learned that at culinary school, as the same instructor had been there for more than thirty years.

To monitor my learning curve, Thomas had me time myself to measure my progress. In addition to breaking down fish, La Tour was also serving Manhattan steaks, the same Manhattans that I watched our chef prepare on my first Lake Powell trip. Thomas showed me how on the large end there was a section of internal sinew that you needed to remove. He described it as a "half-pipe," cutting the large end off so the sinew would be visible and removed. Another four to five portions would still be salvageable.

During my first year at La Tour, our staff, once again, had a lot of maturing to do. While I felt I had outgrown it, the rest of the staff was still heavily into drugs. Particularly the industry's drug of choice: cocaine. I knew it and Chef Paul knew it. Neither of us were idiots. We'd been around a long time. At this point, though, I was past that stage and ready to take my profession seriously. Because drugs were such a big part of the industry, I knew there was not much I could do about it.

Marijuana was something I never truly enjoyed. I couldn't function on it. I knew a lot of my staff members were smoking on the job. I often had to yell out the back door, telling them to "get back in the fucking kitchen." I'd had a long background of being a complete fuckup, especially in my early years. My past was far from being a parent's or boss's dream. So I was understanding.

But I was pissed when I couldn't find them in the kitchen, and I knew where they were. I didn't have time to leave the kitchen to track them down. It became even more evident when the condo owners behind the restaurant found an apple that had been used as a smoking utensil. Chef Paul was especially upset with the news. Those condos were private property—and it was an apple! Where do you think that apple came from?

Chef Paul probably wouldn't be too pleased to hear it, but I actually instructed the cooks to smoke on the line and blow it out the exhaust, urging them to try to be at least a little discreet. I much preferred to at least know where they were. One afternoon, Joe and I were in the walk-in down in the parking garage and our general manager, Chad, walked down, explaining how he thought they might be smoking weed in the kitchen. I later learned that one of the cooks was smoking a bowl with our food runner. Chad had caught the food runner behind the line just as he sucked in a big hit off a bowl. With the smoke still in his mouth, Chad confronted him, and the food runner exhaled directly in Chad's face. So he "thought" they were smoking weed? It seemed quite obvious to me.

The food runner got fired. I, however, kept the cook. After all, he had done exactly what I had instructed him to do. He just wasn't as discreet as I had hoped for. My pot-smoking staff had actually become quite helpful, though. That summer, my long-time friend—long enough to consider my sister—came in for dinner. Jen Jen, Popeye's daughter, was there with a few of her girlfriends. I decided I wanted to take care of them and started them off with some of my favorite appetizers. One was a cold-smoked tuna poke, served in a small mason jar filled with smoke. The presentation was the biggest "wow" factor of the dish. However, our smoking gun was broken, and we had no backup. As we were brainstorming a solution, my line cook, Ian, came up with the idea of making a gravity bong. I had never been much of a smoker, so the concept was new to me. As it turned out, it was actually quite simple, involving the basic understanding of gravity. We cut out the large bottom of a plastic bottle, and on the small opening we constructed a bowl out of aluminum foil. With lit wood chips in the bowl, we submerged the base of the bottle in a bucket of water. As we pulled the bottle out, it caused a vacuum that filled the bottle with smoke. We fanned the smoke into the jar. For any other guests, I would have just eighty-sixed the dish, but Jen Jen was special. My friends and family have always been my biggest VIPs.

Ian was one of my favorite cooks, and although not the cleanest or most organized worker, I would consider him my most knowledgeable and dedicated. I could tell Ian really want- ed to be a chef. I felt bad for him, because he had a serious disease that was holding him back. Ian had Crohn's disease, a disease I knew almost nothing about. Randomly in the middle of service, Ian would say he thought he shat himself. He said it with a smile on his face, so I never took him too seriously. I just yelled at him to toughen up. There were times I believe, in fact, he did shit himself, as work was too busy to allow him time to go to the bathroom.

La Tour would often host large parties, serving pre-fixed menus. Even if it was my scheduled day off, Thomas would re- quest that I be there to assist him. Often Thomas was able to handle the situation himself, but he at least liked that I would be there to observe. Both Thomas and Chef Paul were dedicated, and a sinking ship was never acceptable. I was also dedicated, so whenever I was needed, I was more than willing to assist.

One night in particular numerous amounts of bad luck struck during busy dinner service. Ian's Crohn's disease hit him hard, and he had to leave. I had been enjoying an evening of cocktails at Friday Afternoon Club down the road at the Westin in Avon when my phone rang. Thomas said the ship was, in fact, sinking, and I needed to get to La Tour as quickly as possible. Although only about ten miles down the road, since I don't drive, it was an hour-long bus ride away. Maybe longer. I had barely missed the bus and was unable to get to the restaurant in time. The damage was done: long ticket times, incomplete orders went out, and numerous complaints resulted in comped meals. Our ship had hit the bottom of the sea.

During my first summer as the sous chef, I was probably the toughest to work with. I was still developing my leadership skills. Thomas pulled me aside one afternoon and explained to me how he and Chef Paul each had their own way of leading a kitch-en. The statement couldn't have been more accurate. Chef Paul was hard-nosed and old school. His way or the highway. He would very much let everyone know he was the chef. Chef Paul was also one of the most quotable of any chef I have ever met. An unsuspecting cook would be cutting chives, and he would pick up a single chive and ask the cook, "What's this?" The cook would respond, "It's a chive, chef." Chef Paul would answer, "No. It's money. My money," a quick reminder of reality.

I was helping with desserts one night. I scooped out ice cream to put in the bowl. The scoop was nice, yet not perfectly smooth. The water for the scoop was not warm enough. I used the scoop anyway, resulting in the ice cream sticking—just a little. Chef Paul heard me instruct my assistant to hide the minor imperfections of the scoop as he garnished. Chef Paul's response: "Hey! Show some fucking skill." His favorite word was, in fact, "fuck." And I loved that about him. "Fuck" was my favorite word, as well. I enjoyed the question, "Why do you have to talk like that? It's offensive." Well, yeah, that was the point. if it wasn't offensive, the point wouldn't come across as strong. Cursing like a sailor didn't even compare to cursing like a chef, especially in the La Tour kitchen. I enjoyed Chef Paul's intensity, and his standards in the kitchen could not be matched. I related to him. Although I was not trying to replicate him, I was trying to maintain his high standards.

Thomas, however, led the kitchen completely differently. He was a people person and extremely nurturing. Thomas could always understand the cooks' needs and desires. Add that to his understanding of how to put them in positions where they could be successful. The two chefs had perfectly contrasting styles. I had the opportunity to learn from both of them.

Noah was assigned to our meat station. I was overly tough on Noah, because he was a cocky cook. I hated cockiness; you can't get better if you think you're the best. Noah also liked to dance. He would be dancing on the line, and I'd yell at him, "If you're going to dance, you need to clock out first." I was only halfway joking. I did want professionalism and concentration while he was at work. He never seemed focused. In Vendetta's, we played loud music during service, and it was a dance party back there. But at La Tour, there was no stereo. It was all business. That was the way I preferred things these days, with my party days behind me—at least when it came to work. After work was a different story.

One night, our staff had all gathered at The George after

service. We were drinking shots of tequila—the booze of choice for a wild time. Our cute, young hostess (barely over the legal drinking age) was there and flashed her boobs. A couple who had eaten at La Tour earlier that evening saw. They wrote a bad review on TripAdvisor. The review read, "Everything was great, until we saw the hostess flashing her boobs at the bar." Everyone was off the clock and even off the property, so it shouldn't have mattered, right? Wrong. I realized we represented La Tour. We would be judged no matter where we went. We had the review removed, as it damaged the girl's reputation while having nothing to do with the restaurant, but I realized, although not necessarily fair, our guests had the right to judge me no matter the circumstances. I was obligated to act as a professional at all times—not necessarily my forte.

Noah, an experienced cook, expressed interest in creating a foie gras special. Thomas encouraged me to help Noah get more involved, because his confidence/cockiness showed that being involved would make him happy. Noah seemed quite set on doing something with carbonated blueberries. I liked the idea, so I was more than willing to help him work on creating something we could serve. I had never actually done it before, but a previous cook told me that La Tour had once done a dish using carbonated berries and the technique had a dramatic presentation.

I had heard of a couple of different ways to go about it. A special canister filled with berries would be compressed with a carbon dioxide cartridge. As the canister would be opened table-side, the foamy, carbonated berries would spill out onto the dish, creating an explosion of berry goodness.

The other idea I had heard of was using dry ice. Dry ice

is a solid form of carbon dioxide. In a sealed container, as the ice melted, the contents of the container would then absorb the carbon dioxide. Not only did the canister idea sound a lot more impressive, I had also purchased my own personal canister. So I invited Noah over to my house to experiment. Although we never succeeded in creating a dish worthy of serving at La Tour, my intentions were to just let Noah know his ideas were being heard.

Toward the end of summer, my suspicions that Joe was preparing to leave La Tour had been confirmed. Joe put in his notice and was moving on. Joe was the last of my predecessors in the La Tour kitchen. Now it was just me and Thomas.

My first full year at La Tour was coming to an end. And during this time, I had seen the restaurant go through a massive chef turnover. From executive chefs, executive sous chefs, and sous chefs, I could count six chefs just off the top of my head who had left. Joe would make the seventh.

It wasn't just the chefs who were leaving. It was the line cooks, too. Line cooks who had been there far too long, many who had become complacent and stuck in their ways. From my viewpoint, it looked like the old ways weren't working anymore. It was apparent that La Tour was about to begin a new era. I was excited.

# Chapter 14:

## A New Era

A month or so had passed since Joe's departure. Thomas's immense dedication had me believing that we were preparing to take La Tour to the next level. I was wrong. After summer ended, the restaurant business slowed down. I was once again alone downstairs in our prep room working, and just as he had done a few months earlier, Thomas casually struck up a conversation with me.

In a somber tone, he said, "I've already told Chef Paul, I've already told Lourdes, I've told the other managers, and now I'm telling you." I was the last to find out: Chef Thomas was quitting. The news came as a huge shock, and I was crushed—although I should have known. Thomas had no intentions of ever relocating his family to Vail. With small children, why would he make them move to a new school? It was, after all, the end of summer, and the new school year was starting. And no job, especially a chef position, is worth leaving your family for. Then there was his email address: "thegoodshepherd." I should have seen it as a sign his departure was inevitable. Thomas was indeed a good shepherd, a saint. Exactly what I needed.

I'm not sure how long Chef Paul had known of Thomas's inevitable departure, but it seemed as though he already had a plan in place. Chef Paul was promoting two of our cooks to be sous chefs. There was Lexi, in her early to mid-twenties, in-experienced but competent and more than willing to learn. The predominantly male kitchen staff referred to her as "Sexy Lexi." She owned and loved the nickname.

The other lucky soul (or some might think unlucky, considering the high stress of the job) to get the promotion was Toby. Toby was the complete opposite of Sexy Lexi. Not only was Toby a man, but a man in his early to mid-forties. Nobody in the kitchen was calling Toby sexy.

In addition to the recent promotions, Chef Paul was bringing back two of his former sous chefs. One was Brian. I had known him for a long time since his earliest days in the industry. Brian essentially developed his career working his way up the ranks in the La Tour kitchen. He had since relocated to Denver and was the executive chef at the Berkshire. Now having executive chef experience, Chef Paul was bringing him back to head the kitchen at La Tour. In addition to Brian, Chef Paul recruited AJ, another former sous, to be our chef de cuisine. He had been living in California and working in a ramen joint his friend had opened.

The five of us, with Chef Paul making it six, now had the strongest—or at least the biggest—culinary leadership team a restaurant this size could ever dream of. I was beginning to sense Chef Paul's renewed energy for the industry and La Tour, which was his baby. La Tour was, indeed, starting its new era. During the Chef Thomas era, Chef Paul was rarely in the kitchen, as he had confidence that it was in good hands. Still, he never took his mind off of the restaurant.

Beginning with my promotion, Chef Paul began requiring a weekly inventory report rather than the restaurant standard of a monthly report. This way, he could dissect the tiniest of fluctuation of the restaurant's profits. As a sous chef, I wasn't too involved in our numbers. I was trying to ease into the sous chef position. Joe did the main inventory downstairs in our walk-ins and dry storage, while I did the inventory upstairs in our main kitchen.

I tried to accomplish as much of the inventory as possible during service on expo. Unfortunately, much of the inventory needed to wait, as we would go through product throughout the night. I wanted to do all the inventory myself, because I wanted the numbers to be accurate. If our numbers weren't accurate, or I didn't know what they were, I wouldn't be able to order and work with the ingredients I wanted to. Accuracy was important. I didn't trust my cooks; why would they care? Before I had been promoted, Thomas had asked, "Why is all the inventory in different handwriting?" I agreed with him. How could it be accurate or at least consistent with different people doing it, especially when most of what they were doing was eyeballed?

With Thomas's departure, Chef Paul once again became heavily involved with the operations of the kitchen, everything from menu development, restaurant promotional activities, and even some catered events. Since we had such a large restaurant leadership team, I was also less needed in the kitchen. When it had been primarily Thomas and me, I was always the one in the kitchen.

Thomas had just returned from working an event down the road for the Roundup River Ranch, a nonprofit organization. The event was held outside in a field and was a large social gathering. When he got back to La Tour, dinner service was beginning. I asked Thomas how the event went.

"It was fun. Good people-watching. But you're more valuable

in the kitchen," he said.

I felt the same way. Sometimes, though, I wished I had the time to get out a little more.

After six months, according to my contract, I was owed a week of paid vacation. I refused to take the time off, as our staff was limited. I wondered who was there to work my shifts? Chef Paul? After running La Tour for as long as he had, I felt he needed the time off more than I did. And honestly, I wanted to be there. I was eager to be at work, and I had big aspirations. I didn't want the restaurant to take any steps backward.

Chef Paul was beginning to plan many special events. The first event I remember him planning was a ProStart reunion fundraiser dinner. It had been years since Chef Paul had retired from mentoring the team and now many of his past students had developed into accomplished chefs and restaurateurs. Chef Paul decided it would be a good time to finally reunite with his past students. Inviting five of his past students into the tiny La Tour kitchen seemed like a challenge all in itself. So I was given the night off. Although a night off is always nice, I felt as though I was missing out on something special.

The menu they were serving began with a series of hors d'oeuvres during a reception, with special cocktails created for the event, followed by a five-course meal, all with wine pairings, each chef responsible for one of the courses. It sounded like an amazing dinner, with the money going back to the Battle Mountain ProStart program—back to the industry I loved. Although I had the urge to stop in, I figured with so much going on, as an employee, I didn't want to get in the way.

At the restaurant, some of our best line cooks were a trio of Mexicans, all about five-foot-two, little guys perfect for the size of our tiny line. They were great cooks and hard workers. I never had any complaints about them, although communication could be tough sometimes, because they didn't all speak English fluently. I didn't mind; I loved having an international staff. That trio rarely gave me attitude, and they could put food out fast.

One busy night, a large party of around ten guests arrived. As I was placing their food on the cart to be taken out to the dining room, I noticed a chicken was missing.

I yelled at the line, "Hey! You got a chicken coming?"

The cook yelled back, "You're not telling me what ticket!"

I pulled the ticket down, shoved it in his face, and yelled, "Right fucking here. Read your god damn fucking ticket!"

As most of the food was already on the cart, I needed it fast. Before I even put the ticket back up, the chicken was in the window.

After service, a friend of mine was sitting at the bar.

"Busy night," he said. He had easily heard me yelling at my staff.

I looked frustrated and just shook my head. As I returned to the kitchen, the same cook who just minutes ago I'd gone off on, said, "Good job tonight, chef."

I honestly loved and respected that staff. Even after they stopped working for me, they still called me chef.

Chef Paul had an unwritten rule that whenever we did over a hundred covers he would buy the kitchen staff a round of drinks. I didn't go by this rule. I considered the round of drinks an award for a job well done. I didn't necessarily feel my cooks always did a good job, even when serving a hundred guests. Furthermore, sometimes fifty guests could be a tougher night of service than a hundred.

The cooks were aware of Chef Paul's rule and would often help themselves to a drink at the bar after a busy night. This pissed me off. I had to tell the bartenders they weren't allowed to comp the kitchen drinks. I wanted the round of drinks to actually be an award that they needed to earn, something to motivate staff to improve. I wasn't trying to hand out "participation trophies." With my favorite trio from south of the border, I never had that problem. They always deserved a round. In addition to being hardworking, they were mentally and physically prepared for service.

We finally had a strong staff, so I decided it was time to take advantage of the paid vacation time I was owed. I was in search of new culinary inspiration. Once again, I planned on traveling for food, just not at the level of Geranium. After searching for affordable flights I had decided on two established culinary destinations, Las Vegas and San Francisco. I knew in Las Vegas, all I needed to do was walk down the strip and I would see a great restaurant worth trying.

I needed to do a little research for San Francisco, however. I knew about most of the world-renowned, Michelin-starred restaurants, such as Saison and Manresa. I also knew I couldn't afford that type of dinner. I still had massive credit card debt from Europe. Upon further research, I learned of a Thai restaurant, Kin Khao, that had recently received its first Michelin star. At only $70 for a seven-course tasting menu, I could afford to try it out. Plus, a Michelin star in Thai food! I'd never heard of that before.

After booking my flight, I began searching hotel rooms. The flights were so cheap I figured finding a room shouldn't be a problem; I could even splurge a little. Not being much of a football fan, I had no idea that the stupid Super Bowl was going on while I was there. Finding a room turned out to be more difficult than I expected, but I eventually found one.

In San Francisco, I walked down to the pier and was greeted by beautiful views of the bay and Golden Gate Bridge. A lot of great restaurants were down there, as well. I went to the renowned Slanted Door, along with the Hog Island Oyster Company, then La Mar, and, of course, the Michelin-star Thai restaurant. Upon arriving at Kin Khao, I was actually surprised it had a star. There was nothing magical about the restaurant. Brightly lit with wooden tables, it seemed like an ordinary mid-level restaurant. Although the food was still good, it lacked the magic I witnessed in Europe.

Perhaps I would have better luck in Vegas.

After a quick flight to Vegas, I decided to have dinner at Julian Serrano's tapas restaurant in the Aria Resort and Casino. I wanted to enjoy a somewhat casual dinner, so I sat at the bar. I wasn't thinking of a full meal. I casually ordered one plate at a time, along with a proper wine to go with it. I was creating my own tasting menu.

In my short time at La Tour, I'd developed a basic understanding of wines, so simple wine pairings were easy to make. The bartender must have taken notice and mentioned it to the kitchen. Because by the time I ordered my third course, a rustic pork dish that I paired with an old-world Tempranillo, one of the chefs came out, suggesting another good wine pairing for one of his dishes. This helped me realize that I had truly developed as a chef.

After returning from my vacation, I learned Chef Paul had been planning a high-end catering event in the ritzy Bachelor Gulch neighborhood in the Avon/Beaver Creek area just down the road from Vail. Chef Paul had been planning this event with a local Master Sommelier, Damon. Chef Paul asked me when was the last time I had catered an event. I told him it had been a long time, even though I'd never really done it professionally. I had catered my sister's wedding many years earlier, but it was small and for family only. But it still kind of counted, so I wasn't lying.

Chef Paul always treated his food and overall dining experience with the same care and attention to detail, whether it was served in the restaurant or off-site. All our utensils, plates, and even serviettes needed to be packed and transported.

"Be professional. Use a fucking serviette" was another common Chef Paul quote.

This event was the first time since I arrived at La Tour when I finally witnessed the greatness of Chef Paul's culinary knowledge. Some of the food we served was the best I'd seen the restaurant produce yet. One dish in particular stuck out: the tomato sauce. Yes, simple tomato sauce. He had made the sauce using veal demi-glace. I'd never seen that before. Even coming from an Italian restaurant like Vendetta's, this was a completely new concept and blew my mind. Vendetta's specialized in tomato sauces. We served five or six variations, but none of them used demi-glace. The demi-glace was genius. It added body and a depth of flavor I'd never tasted in a tomato sauce.

We arrived at the house of the catered event. I was in the kitchen getting set up and organized. Chef Paul and Damon went down with our hosts to see his wine collection. The hosts of the party were providing their own wine, which Damon expertly paired with Chef Paul's food. After the successful dinner, we packed up our cars and were leaving.

Chef Paul looked at me and said, "I know he's a doctor, but

he must have invented something, because there was at least a quarter of a million dollars worth of wine in that cellar."

This was when I *really* started to realize what level of a chef he was; we had some high-end clientele.

This summer was the summer I like to refer to as "the summer of wine dinners." I was quickly learning how well-connected Chef Paul was. He knew a lot of winemakers, purveyors, and brand ambassadors.

Once again, Chef Paul chose to team up with Damon for an "Italian" wine dinner at La Tour. It was a special, reservation-only event in a semi-private room. I had the night off, so Chef Paul invited me to stop in and enjoy the dinner he had carefully crafted. It was a Tuesday night, and I was at the weekly free concert being held at Ford Park. While I was enjoying the show, I knew I definitely didn't want to miss this dinner. I called up the host to let them know I was coming, as I was still a good fifteen minutes away and running late. Upon my arrival, Chef Paul, Damon, and Sexy Lexi were sitting at a table already eating. I had a little catching up to do.

When the squab dish arrived, Chef Paul said, "This would be a $50 dish at Robuchon's." He tugged on the tacky brown paper being used as a tablecloth. "It's all because of this shit."

I agreed. You can't be an upscale restaurant if you're too poor for linens.

When the final dish arrived, a house-made tiramisu served in a tall glass, Chef Paul asked the server to pour me a glass of Marsala. The Marsala was a "bonus" wine that wasn't actually offered as a pairing to our other guests. I sipped the wine with the tiramisu and had a revelation. This was the best damn wine pairing I had ever had! Chef Paul, afterward, confessed that it was the exact same wine he used to make the cake. The food was easily of Michelin-star quality.

After the meal, I stood up and gestured toward our tiny kitchen and my favorite trio of Mexicans. In front of Damon, Sexy Lexi, and Chef Paul, I said, "We can compete with the best in the world." And I meant it. I added, "We just don't get the publicity of being in a city."

From that moment on, I continually tried instilling that belief in everyone's heads. Not just with our staff, but to all the locals and tourists passing through town, too. I began promoting the restaurant more than I think anyone ever had. The entire town of Vail was beginning to take notice.

Everything seemed to be going great at La Tour. Our roles were beginning to be defined. Brian, as our executive chef, was almost exclusively an office chef—which was perfectly acceptable. He was good at it. Besides, he was the only one of us who was married. As an office chef, you pretty much get to work your own hours, as long as the computers aren't taken.

The rest of us—well, I guess we just didn't really need to "have lives" outside of work. AJ, being well aware of the dedication needed, had even brought in his own air mattress for the occasional night when he might have to sleep at work. While AJ, Sexy Lexi, and I often alternated between swing shifts, opening, and closing, Toby assumed the role that Joe had previously occupied: Show up around six in the morning to get prep started and set up the line. Lunch was still just an afterthought. All the *mise-en-place* was, of course, downstairs in the walk-in, and those stairs were hell! So I really did appreciate the work Toby and our lunch staff put in. I remember my first winter, I was carrying a double stack of bus tubs with all my mise in them. I slipped on the icy stairs, luckily catching the railing with my armpit and sliding down the rest of the way. I hated those cheese graters.

Around fifteen years earlier, Chef Paul had received his honorary doctorate from the Art Institute of Colorado. This was a rare accomplishment, something I never knew was possible. So in addition to being called "chef," he would also go by "doctor." During one of our manager meetings, Chef Paul stated he was now "Doctor Dad," having all but completely handed over his restaurant to his team of chefs.

With such a large leadership team, I was allowed extra free time to focus on my specials. So this also became the summer where I began working with foie gras a lot. Ever since I'd started at La Tour, the one constant but ever-changing dish on the menu was our seared foie gras. We always served a seared foie gras. Sometimes a cold preparation, as well. Although I'd eaten foie gras in Sweden, I'd never had it sliced and seared like we were serving it at La Tour. It turned out to be probably the most versatile ingredient I'd ever worked with.

I was developing an appreciation for seared foie gras. It's all about the textures. When perfectly cooked—and being cooked perfectly is the key—seared foie gras has the complete range of textures. The seared crust is so thin it's almost more like a skin than a crust. As you dig deeper, the textures continually change, cutting through the melting fat and ending in the al dente bite of the center with a perfect chew. I believe seared is the best way to serve foie gras. But it is easy to fuck up.

Although I was changing the dish constantly, I did have a favorite preparation inspired by the lemon bavarois I had at the wedding in Sweden. I added textual ingredients and a French-spiced watermelon jelly. Not too complicated, but I felt it had it all. If I were to have a signature dish, that would be it. The dish got some good reviews, too. I heard people talking about it all around town. But I thrived on originality. My dishes were con- stantly changing. This kept my job fun and interesting. It's tough to have a signature dish when nothing is ever served more than a couple weeks.

I was working expo for dinner service one night when Noah called in, claiming he had hurt his elbow and couldn't work. I wasn't who he had talked to; otherwise I would have given him some serious shit about it. A hurt elbow was no excuse to miss work.

After I got off work that night, I was at the George having my customary after-work drinks. I saw Noah walk in, just dancing away like it was no big deal. I thought to myself, *"He had to know he would see me here. I'm here every night."* I instantly thought he was trying to take advantage of our "friendship." I don't let people take advantage of me. I was fucking furious. I was ready to kick his ass. It was a free concert night. He wasn't hurt; he just wanted to go to the concert.

I cared about my job and took it seriously, so when it came to work, if someone tried to screw me over, we sure as hell weren't friends anymore. What did he think would happen when he called in sick? Somebody had to cover his ass. As I was sched- uled to expo, that somebody was me. I flipped. We were at the George, so I no longer felt the need to be professional. Since I'd lived in Vail for as long as I had and I was also respected locally in the industry, I felt I had some pull. I said he'd never work in this town again.

By the time I went back to work the next day, I had settled down a bit. Sexy Lexi and Chef Paul were in the office. I calmly explained what had happened and that I wanted to fire Noah. Chef Paul's reaction was simple.

"That's how Noah is," he said.

Yeah, I knew that, too. That was exactly why I wanted to fire him. I wanted dedicated cooks.

Brian happened to be out of town at the time, so Chef Paul suggested that we waited for Brian to get back. When Brian returned, since he had been gone during the incident, he let Noah keep his job.

The very next week Noah called in again. On a free concert night. This time, he claimed he had eaten moldy bread and was sick. That was a terrible excuse, especially for a cook. If you're eating moldy bread, what are you serving our guests? Needless to say, Brian fired him this time.

Noah wasn't the only cook we were beginning to have problems with, so Brian called for a chef meeting. At this meeting, Brian told us we could fire whoever we wanted—just be prepared to cover for them, as he implied we didn't have any replacements. I was fine with that. In Noah's case, I was already covering for him without any notice or warning. I had to adjust my plans last minute, anyway.

Around this time, I overheard AJ say, "We need to get some young cooks in here, straight outta culinary school." So I went on the hunt.

One night, I was enjoying my usual after-work activity of drinking beers at the George. While I was there, sitting right next to me were two young cooks, probably around twenty-two years old, dressed in the old, classic checkered chef pants. They were discussing work, so I asked them if they wanted a job and handed them one of my business cards.

A couple weeks later, one of those chefs, Ally, came into La Tour and spoke to Brian. She mentioned my name and Brian hired her on the spot. Just like that, we at least had one youthful soul in our kitchen. Ally was exactly what I was looking for, too: easily trainable and with a ton of passion.

Soon there was another incident involving one of our cooks, "Q." One night, I saw Q standing in the middle of the parking garage. Naturally assuming she didn't have anything to do, I delegated a job for her. But she passed the job off to one of our other newly hired cooks. I wasn't having it.

"I told *you* to do it," I yelled at her.

We broke into a huge argument. She threatened to leave, as she knew we would be short-staffed.

"Just fucking leave then," I said. She hadn't been much help to begin with.

I didn't have time to argue and went back to work. Tears started falling down her face. Because we'd be short-staffed, it was clear she'd expected me to act like we needed her, and she wanted to feel important. That wasn't how I saw it, though. I saw her as unstable and a liability. She was a military girl. I figured she could handle it. She couldn't.

Our general manager, Chad, overheard everything and tried to settle the situation. The three of us sat in the office, and Chad got Brian on the speakerphone.

"Brian, this is what's going on," Chad said and let Brian listen in on us arguing.

By this point, I was half-ass apologizing, but she wasn't accepting my half-ass apology. I was just saying anything that could possibly make her happy. We had an extremely busy service ahead. And I had a ton of work to do.

In fact, that was exactly why I had told her to just go home; she was a distraction, and I needed to work. I had a very new staff, including Ally, who was scheduled to work sauté for the first time in her entire life. I was prepared for training Ally. She was in at least in a good mental state. Being focused and understaffed is always better than having a distracted staff.

Eventually, the fight resolved, Q agreed to stay, and we were all back in the kitchen manning our stations. Chad approached me while I was setting up expo.

"Are you guys gonna be all right?" he asked.

I was honestly worried. I didn't want to tell Chad that, though. I was going to handle it the best I could in a professional way. I knew I might have to own up and take the heat from Chef Paul if the ship sank.

Staffing this summer was tough. Even my beloved trio of Mexicans left us. None of our new hires were working out. Our kitchen staff was not gelling as a team in any possible sense. I was beginning to get really frustrated. This was not the working environment I was looking for. Not my dream kitchen, where everyone was happy and treated like equals. We lacked professionalism and, quite frankly, it was hell. I didn't think it was ever going to get better.

Then things got worse.

We got hit by some shocking and unexpected news. Brian's wife was pregnant. So Brian decided it would be best for him to move back East so his parents could help raise their newborn. Brian wished he could stay, but putting his family first was best. An obvious choice.

Even though we had some staffing issues, La Tour had been making some huge strides since my arrival. La Tour was, indeed, on its way up. Chef Paul's renewed enthusiasm, in addition to our improved financial situation, was about to bring some much needed dining room upgrades. Starting with the carpets, stained with an unappealing, smeared dark gray from all the heavy foot traffic.

While in California, Chef Paul had also found some nice wooden tabletops to eliminate the need for tablecloths. Since the wood tables were coming from the coast, they needed time to acclimate to Vail's dry climate and elevation and couldn't be replaced immediately. But the word of new tables was a positive sign of things to come.

Although Brian's sudden departure caught us off guard, I wasn't going to let it slow us down. Actually, my ambition and drive grew. I felt more enthusiastic than ever. One night, all of the chefs sat on the floor in our tiny, five-square-foot office, while Chef Paul researched new menu ideas on the computer. Cramped in that little office, but brainstorming as a team, was exactly the environment I had dreamed of: a small team with big ambitions. I could feel the energy, and we truly felt like a team.

Even Toby, primarily responsible for lunch, finally felt like a part of our team. Where there had previously been a disconnect, now Toby was coming up with menu ideas. This was one of the few times when all of the chefs were able to gather at once. La Tour would never close the kitchen between lunch and dinner; we ran service straight through. Never stopping service meant one of us would always be in the kitchen. But at this moment, the restaurant was slow enough that we could all be together.

We also had the addition of a new, young beverage director who had left Elway's to join us. I could tell she had limited knowledge about wine, but she seemed to want to learn. I could sense her enthusiasm, as the two of us were usually the last ones in the restaurant, working the longest hours. Her boyfriend was the sommelier at Elway's, where I assumed they had met.

I was walking through the village one afternoon when I ran into them, so naturally I asked them what they were up to. None of us had to work, so it was a no-brainer that we'd go get drinks together. I'm normally a beer drinker, but since I'd started working at La Tour, I had become somewhat of a wine aficionado. So obviously, if I was with a sommelier and our beverage director, we were going to go somewhere with good wine.

There was a wine bar called Root and Flower that had been open for about a year now, located just behind Vendetta's. When we got to the bar, none of us seemed too picky about what we drank. It was a warm summer day, so we all wanted something refreshing. We all ordered the same dry white wine while we looked over the menu for something to snack on. We decided to share some meatballs. As soon as the meatballs arrived, we wondered what we had been thinking. It was a horrible wine pairing. For being "professionals," we had made a disappointing choice.

After recovering from our terrible meatball-and-white wine pairing, we decided to go have beer on the patio at Pepi's, a nearby Austrian bar. It was going to be a day of barhopping. As we walked by a flower bed, my beverage director started picking weeds. Apparently, she cared about good-looking flowers. But she was holding us back, in addition to creating an awkward situation.

Her boyfriend yelled, "Hey, freak show! Let's go!"

I loved the nickname so much that I began calling her that. She didn't love it as much, but she accepted it with a laugh.

Since it was usually just me and Freak Show working at the restaurant late at night, I felt she was dedicated to her job. So one day, I saw her in the office and asked if she wanted to fly to Vegas and have dinner at Pierre Gagnaire's, a highly acclaimed French chef. His creative flagship restaurant in Paris had three Michelin stars and is often credited as the first restaurant to infuse international cuisines together, like my favorite dish of his: a blend of Russian, Japanese, and French. I had found some cheap flights to Vegas and wanted to check out the restaurant for myself.

AJ, who had recently moved up to fill Brian's vacated position, was sitting next to Freak Show making the schedule and overheard. AJ knew my extreme dedication, and he assumed I wasn't joking.

"What days?" he quickly asked.

I had yet to buy the tickets, but I felt obligated now. He gave me the two days off just before our upcoming wine dinner.

Freak Show, on the other hand, thought I was joking and declined to join me; she underestimated my extreme dedication. But I wasn't joking. I went home and booked my trip.

# Chapter 15:

## Don't Do It by the Books

Using my only two days off that week, I flew to Vegas. Although I had taken the trip to San Francisco the previous year for a casual food trip, this was my first serious food trip since Europe. I only had two days, and I was ready to spend some money on food.

After checking into the hotel, I passed by a clothing store on my way to my room. Although I did have some nice clothes with me, I decided I wanted something nicer. I picked out a nice shirt and some pants, not a full suit. But as I was checking out, the lady asked, "What's the suit for?"

"I'm having dinner at Pierre Gagnaire's," I told her. I don't think she knew who Pierre Gagnaire was, and by the expression on her face, I was pretty sure she wasn't accustomed to someone buying nice clothes just to go have dinner. Either way, since I was in Vegas for such a short time, I wasn't planning on spending it in a hotel.

I really only had time for two meals on this trip, so I decided I should check out another one of my chef idol's restaurants. There are a lot of options in Vegas, but I settled on Thomas Keller's Bouchon, since he was one of the first chefs to inspire me with his *French Laundry cookbook*.

Bouchon in the Venetian is a bistro (which in France means

"good," just not fancy), so it's pretty casual. I sat at the bar and ordered the salmon rillettes and the ham and cheese sandwich.

"We don't have a ham and cheese sandwich," the bartender said. Although he was American, I guess he still wanted me to use my best French.

So I rephrased it. "Sorry, the *croque monsieur*."

I always like sitting at bars, because there's no place for your server to hide, which makes it easy to have a conversation. We had a good talk, and he recommended a lot of other restaurants. As he became more comfortable, he started to bitch about how lazy the servers were.

I casually responded, "Yeah, that mirror behind the bar is fucking disgusting." Because it was.

I was enjoying what was a great lunch served on nice, shiny white plates with the Bouchon logo written on them, exactly like in Thomas Keller's cookbooks. The dusty mirror was actually affecting my enjoyment of the meal. Making it worse, he was complaining about lazy servers, which I know is common—but I didn't want to hear it. He wasn't working that hard either. That damn mirror hadn't been cleaned in a year, yet he had time to talk to me and bitch about others.

I had a somewhat late dinner reservation for Gagnaire's, which had given me plenty of time to build up an appetite. After a couple big beers at Guy Fieri's for happy hour, I went back to the hotel to get ready for dinner. I didn't want to walk all the way back to the then-Mandarin Oriental, where Pierre Gagnaire's was located, so I took a cab. After arriving at the Mandarin, I took the elevator to the twenty-third floor, which took me directly to the restaurant. The host then promptly sat me at a nice table overlooking the strip with the partially visible kitchen at my back.

As the server was handing me my menu, I already knew what I was planning on ordering. I was there to have the best they had to offer. At least food-wise. They also offered some ridiculously expensive wine pairing that was nowhere near my budget. But because of Chef Paul, I was hooked on wine pairings. So I ordered the seven-course menu with the standard wine pairing.

They started me off with what they were simply calling "on the table:" about five different offerings of snack-sized bites. These snacks actually reminded me a lot of what I had at Geranium—tiny bites that showcased a ton of mysterious and creative techniques. However, the rest of the meal was unbelievably underwhelming. They served none of the dishes that had made Pierre Gagnaire famous. I owned Pierre Gagnaire's cookbook, Pierre Gagnaire: *Reinventing French Cuisine*. He was doing "French fusion" way before "fusion" was even a culinary term. His cookbook showed the years his dishes were created, dating back to the early eighties. I was extremely disappointed that the food served now was nothing like he'd made nearly forty years earlier.

As I consumed my very expensive meal, it became obvious to the manager and server that I was in the industry. I made simple comments about the wine and foie gras pairing. Knowing how the foie needed to be marinated, I mentioned to the server that it tasted like they used the same wine in preparing the foie gras terrine. Working with Chef Paul, things like that became quite obvious to me. As the server delivered my escargot, he mentioned how he didn't like them because they were too salty. I replied with, "They're probably the exact same ones we get, from Burgundy, straight from a can. They just need to rinse them off first."

After such comments, the chef wanted to meet me. So I was invited into the kitchen. The manager escorted me down a skinny hallway past a tall stack of glass racks. My first impression was, *"Wow, this kitchen really isn't that big for being in Vegas."* I was expecting something more glamorous, considering the city.

After a brief conversation with the chef, I was offered a coffee. I declined the offer and replied, "I need to catch a really early flight to get back for my own wine dinner."

The manager agreed. "Yeah, you probably want to get some sleep."

It didn't matter, though. I couldn't sleep anyway. Around eight in the morning, I flew back to Denver and caught a shuttle back to Vail. By the time I got home, it was already afternoon, so I went straight to work and started preparing for the wine dinner.

A couple weeks later, I heard that one of the youngest master sommeliers in the world, one with Michelin-star credentials from his time in California, was joining our team. His name was Roland. This was a rare opportunity, as there are very few master sommeliers in the entire world. Including the special dinners I had worked with Damon on, I now had the pleasure to work with a second master sommelier. I was thrilled to hear this news, because I strongly felt our front of house needed some solid leadership. The kitchen was pretty strong, but the front needed a leader to match the kitchen's dedication.

Shortly afterward, I learned we were getting a new chef de cuisine, too. Tyson had recently moved to Vail from Wilmington, North Carolina. Although I still had yet to meet Tyson, I could judge by AJ's excitement that Tyson had a ton of experience. With the addition of these two, the excitement levels at La Tour were at an all-time high.

Everyone in Vail was preparing for exciting things at La Tour. We had by far the strongest team I had seen. I was also beginning to see a new pattern with Chef Paul. He liked to show the new chefs the level his restaurant was at. Chef Paul asked Tyson to help him with his next catering event. As Chef Paul was preparing his signature scallop en croute dish, I watched him as he was shaving what looked to be an extremely excessive amount of black truffles. I asked him about it.

He shrugged his shoulders. "It's fourteen hundred dollars a head," he said.

*"Damn!"* I thought to myself. *"Go ahead and do whatever the hell you want then. Shit, give 'em that entire truffle."* It was a charity dinner, after all, at a private residence, benefitting Roundup River Ranch.

Chef Paul's specialty was really in his use of high-end ingredients. I had never known of a chef who would work as hard as Chef Paul when it came to sourcing ingredients. I know, everyone raves about farm-to-table restaurants, but I've always considered farm-to-table as something that should go without saying. Restaurants should always be farm-to-table. It's obviously fresher, but it is also cheaper because you can cut out the middleman.

La Tour was farm-to-table, but because of our level, our "farm" was all over the world, namely Spain and France, in addition to the pork Secreto from the Iberian Peninsula. We were also getting European sea bass from one of the most sustainable fish farms in the world, Veta la Palma. These European sea bass, known as Lupe de Mer, were being shipped overnight directly to the restaurant. The farm would wait for our order, then once they knew our demand, catch, kill, and ship them directly to us. The fish would not only still have the scales, but also the guts.

They were a pain in the ass to clean, but I felt we had a strong enough staff for it not to be an issue. The minimum number of chefs we had during dinner service was two, but often there would be three of us. This allowed for one of the chefs to pretty much stay in the prep room all night. Our butchery this winter was the most labor-intensive of my entire time at La Tour. Several nights in particular, I pulled all-nighters in our prep room just because I was sick of being in the weeds. Being behind added unwanted stress. So I stayed very late, often leaving just before our opening chef would arrive.

One night around three in the morning, I was walking home down the dark frontage road when a bright spotlight hit me. The police were looking for a suspect who had been in a fight earlier that night. When they approached me, I explained I was a chef at La Tour and I was just leaving work. Nervous from the time I had been tased and arrested under similar circumstances, I quickly asked them if they would like to see my ID. I handed them my ID, along with a business card. It wasn't that I was scared of being tased or going to jail. I was nervous because I knew I couldn't afford to get arrested. It was peak season, and I needed to be at work the next day. La Tour needed me. Luckily, after a quick look at my ID, they sent me on my way. Unlike my previous encounter with the police, this time the cops were friendly, even offering me a ride the rest of the way home.

Our large staff allowed us to make staff meals, which I preferred to call family meals, a larger priority. For these pre-shift meals, the staff sat down to eat together, although the kitchen staff often had to miss or eat while standing because they were so busy prepping. I have always lived by the "nothing-goes-to-waste" attitude. I would often find time to grind up meat scraps or even prepare the scraps for braising. I saved fish scraps to be used in seafood soups or made into mousse. I didn't throw anything away.

I would kit up "family meals" a day or two in advance, leaving detailed instructions for the opening chef on how to cook them. My meal kits, similar to the pre-prepped kind the public can buy to make at home, were used for our regular staff gatherings. They came with ingredients cut, spice packets mixed, and liquids already measured. Instructions to prepare were easy, sometimes as simple as boiling water and putting everything into the oven. You'd be surprised; not all chefs know how to cook without a recipe. My goal was to ensure my staff ate a good meal.

I fully believe if you can't cook well for your work "family," you'll never be able to cook well for the hundreds of paying guests you never even get to see. Family meals were taken seriously and thoughtfully crafted. I was on a mission to make La Tour's staff experience the envy of every other restaurant in town.

I was still following Geranium on social media. When they posted a picture of the whole team eating together in the park, I wanted that for La Tour. There's nothing better than being able to sit together as a family and enjoy a meal, so I made that a priority. I wanted to sit down, front and back of house, as a family and eat.

As I got to know Tyson, I began to understand why AJ was so excited he had joined the team. Tyson did have a ton of experience. More than any of the rest of us. And Tyson was book smart—actually beyond book smart when it came to food. Tyson spoke of his massive book collection that far exceeded mine. My collection had slowed once I learned the basics, and I became reliant on inspiration; this was why I traveled. Tyson didn't travel nearly as much as me, but he read. Tyson also knew technology and new-school techniques.

Chef Paul was as old-school as you could get. With him, you really needed to know how to cook with fire. We were the lowest-tech kitchen around. When I first started at La Tour, we didn't have a deep fryer. In fact, we didn't even have a fryer thermometer. Chef Paul instructed us to drop popcorn in a pot of oil, and when it popped we were at 350. That's when we knew we could start frying.

With Tyson, however, it was all technology. Tyson brought in his own chamber vacuum sealer, along with his own thermal circulator that could precisely maintain the temperature of water. With Tyson's help, La Tour was finally leaving the eighties! When it came to food, Tyson's passion was with molecular gastronomy; he often called himself a geek or nerd. I was just beginning to experiment with molecular gastronomy. Tyson had already done many of the experiments I was working on. I was preparing to pick his brain.

Tyson was married with two kids, a teenage son and a younger, pre-teen daughter. After only about a week of working together, I knew I was going to get along well with Tyson. I began to get acquainted with his family better, too. I saw him out with his wife at the upscale bowling alley, Bol, right across the street from La Tour, and they were sitting at a table. Tyson had told me it was his wife's birthday—a celebration. The first thing that comes to my mind when I think "celebration" is champagne. So without even asking, I went to the bar and ordered a bottle. The three of us enjoyed our champagne, while I got to know his wife.

I felt they had good heads on their shoulders. Tyson would often talk to me about his parenting style, a style of parenting I would like to think I'd use, as well. He was laid back, but he would also let his kids know he was the boss. There were days when we needed extra help in the kitchen, usually something like washing dishes. The rest of us would be all stressing, but Tyson would calm us down saying, "Don't worry about it." He'd then get on the phone and call up his son to help.

I told Tyson about my travels through Europe and Copenhagen, and he showed me his Instagram. I didn't have an Instagram. I rarely even got a picture of many of my dishes, or I'd take a quick one mid-service while the dish was in the window. But Tyson loved taking pictures of his food. While he was showing me his Instagram, he mentioned how surprised and thrilled he was when he noticed chef René Redzepi from Noma was following him. Tyson had obviously done some great things in the past. He was also pretty well known in the culinary world back in Wilmington, competing in culinary competitions and making local television appearances.

Then in the spring, Tyson's friend, Christy, decided to move out to Vail. He not only let her stay in his house, but he also got her a job at La Tour. Since Christy was new in town, she wanted to see what Sweet Basil was all about; Sweet Basil was Vail's most popular and established restaurant. I always enjoy eating out, so I offered to go with her. Everyone knew me at Sweet Basil, but in those cases, it can go both ways: You can either get great service because they know you or you can get horrible service because they know you. On this particular night, we got the latter. I wasn't going to say anything (that's not my style), but Christy, new to town, had no problem complaining. It did result in free dessert, and we both opted for glasses of ten-year Tawny.

Whereas Christy was vividly upset, I was calmly upset. I questioned whether the server knew who I was. Did he not understand my dedication to the industry? Did he not understand I travel the world for the best restaurants, specifically to judge them? Did he not expect me to tell the entire town about my bad experience? I never asked or even expected to be treated as a VIP, but the server should have been prepared for the consequences.

From what I heard, the manager laid into him pretty good. Turned out, the server did know who I was, and when I saw him later at the bar, he asked, "Were you on a date?" The answer was no, but the question was irrelevant. If a chef is out to dinner, you can be almost certain the person they are with is someone of importance. Especially if you don't know who the guest is. Chefs generally only associate with others in the industry and are usually well connected.

One of the reasons I liked Christy so much was she didn't mind the occasional cuss word. One Sunday, Christy was working brunch. It was a slow day so she was about to get cut. She sent me a text to see if I wanted to have lunch with her. I suggested we meet up at La Botega to enjoy lunch on the sunny patio.

During lunch, we talked about work, of course. Christy was still new to La Tour, so I was explaining my leadership style and how I treated my staff. Our line cook, Eric, just so happened to be a prime example. I explained to Christy what I thought of Eric.

"I like Eric, but he needs to toughen the fuck up and stop being a such a fucking pussy and get his fucking shit together," I said, among many other creatively inappropriate words. I went off for a while. Eventually, I calmed down and started to carefully describe what I meant by "pussy."

As it was a Sunday morning, a nice couple sitting next to us could hear every word. The gentleman got up and kindly asked me to not continue our conversation. He was offended by the language. Although we weren't at La Tour, I still felt like apologizing for disrupting their meal. So as we were leaving, I gave them a sincere apology. The couple did deserve to enjoy a pleasant meal, and having a meal on a sunny patio is one of the greatest joys in life. My conversation was inappropriate; I had grown heated about work and completely lost my composure.

Chef Thomas had told me I needed to develop my own leadership style. I felt I had. I originally thought I was going to find a balance between Chef Paul and Thomas. If I was going to find that balance at all, it wasn't going to happen at La Tour. La Tour needed a tough chef. I wasn't trying to be Chef Paul either, though. I had already been greatly influenced by Popeye, and I had my own way of yelling at people. Popeye had toughened me up, and I greatly appreciated that; I needed to toughen up. Now it was my turn. I needed to toughen up my staff.

Often, sous chefs think of their job as babysitting. I made damn sure everyone knew I wasn't babysitting. I liked to say I was turning boys into men, just like Popeye had turned me into a man. Although I never stole his "rip-your-fucking-head-off" line, I did threaten to throw them "down the fucking stairs." I also had no problem telling them to their face to toughen the fuck up.

Eric reminded me of myself when I was young, which was why I liked him the most. But Eric was a Millennial.

You can't control when you're born. My love for the eighties always had me wishing I was born ten years earlier. After I burned my house down, I felt like I had aged ten years overnight, so in some ways, I felt older than I was.

The older generations often complain about Millennials, but we were the ones who raised them that way. My generation is to be blamed. So if we shaped them to begin with, I thought, why couldn't we change them? Toughening up Eric became my micro mission. I knew the other chefs didn't like him, but he was exactly what I was looking for. I could yell at him all I wanted, and he'd never cry and walk out, like a lot of other staff did. Never Eric, though. So I had a lot of respect for him.

All of the chefs yelled at Eric, but the biggest difference was how we would yell at him. I always yelled at Eric to do shit. Other chefs yelled at him how he should do shit. This pissed me off, probably more than anything. There was a big difference. Telling someone how to do something holds them back, hindering their growth. By yelling at Eric to simply do the thing was making him a man. He would actually have to think, use his brain, and learn. And Eric wanted to use his brain. Just like me, he didn't like being told exactly what to do (the main reason I hated school). Telling Eric how to do things was babysitting, keeping him from becoming self-sufficient. Eric needed to grow up, and I believed he could. The other chefs just didn't trust him and never gave him a chance. That pissed me off the most—not giving someone a chance.

Once while I was cleaning, Scooby had told me, "Now Paul, there's more than one way to do things." Scooby was, in fact, right. I had been cleaning, "doing it by the books." But that was essentially not thinking. This was an important lesson for me to learn, because at the time I was reading a lot of books. I needed to be innovative, freethinking, and develop my own style. It was natural and easier to copy what other proven chefs had already done. When I stopped doing things "by the book," I began to trust my own palate and became creative.

This industry is all about people. The objective is simple: Make people happy. The people you cater to, the people you work with, and the people you work for. If everyone is happy, you are a success. Helping everyone become a success is the main goal of a leader. In order for everyone to be successful and happy, you need to understand them, and everyone is different.

Thomas was right in understanding the need to nurture people. However, everyone needs a different kind of "nurturing." Having a large staff turnover, in my opinion, is a sign of poor leadership. Especially at a restaurant of La Tour's caliber; people wanted to work there. They came to La Tour. All leadership needed to do was not make it completely suck for them. Chefs often waste their energy looking for the perfect staff. I decided to let them come to me, and then turn them into the perfect staff.

Take Manny and his cracker dilemma. I wanted to make sure it looked simple; he needed to build his confidence. Manny wanted me to hold his hand and show him step by step. He feared being yelled at.

On the other hand, Eric was much like me when I first got in the industry: a punk on the outside but a baby on the inside. Eric was stubborn, and I needed to beat into his head that he could do it without me—he had to do it without me.

Both Manny and Eric were young kids. Manny could make a simple cracker. He was just too scared to. Eric wasn't scared of fucking up and being yelled at. He didn't even have to fuck up. He was already being yelled at just for not following instructions. Two opposite characters could succeed in the La Tour kitchen.

One night I was working expo, and Alanna was our front-of-house manager. Two guys ordered a split portion of lamb. One of the guests complained about his half being overcooked. I was in a good mood and feeling generous, so I gladly cooked a new "half" order of lamb. I'm pretty sure the other diner was just joking or probably flirting with Alanna when he said, "I'll have the other half. It's just going to waste anyway."

I decided to personally deliver the properly cooked lamb to the guest who had complained. This was a pretty common gesture for me; I liked to ensure the guest was happy, especially after a problem. I felt I understood our food better than anyone in the restaurant, so I felt more qualified to defend the food or correct the food if it was required. I also felt I could read and understand the guests better than our entire staff. After inquiring if the new lamb was to his liking, the guest said it was perfect. He then went on to explain how the first one was just a tad over. It seemed like he wasn't expecting the chef to personally bring his food. The guests were nice and understanding, so I brought them the extra piece of lamb.

"It's generally not our policy, but here. Enjoy!" I said. Needless to say, they were thrilled.

After they left, I found out that Alanna had comped the dish. I felt the extra portion of lamb was a comp in itself. Considering how they acted when I was at their table, I felt they had taken advantage of our young manager.

Now I was no longer in a good mood. I was furious and raced out of the restaurant looking for them. They were nowhere to be seen, which was actually a good thing. I don't know what I would have done if I had seen them. But as I returned to the restaurant, I saw Alanna crying, which made me feel terrible. I definitely hadn't meant to make her cry; I was actually trying to have her back. I wasn't going to let anybody take advantage of our young staff.

The next day when I saw Chad, he told me he didn't want me talking to our guests anymore. We clearly had different ways of running a restaurant. I had interacted with many guests over the last few years; they often loved seeing the chef. I told Chad I had been "very professional" when talking to the customers the day before.

"I'm sure you were," he said sincerely.

I felt the need to defend myself. "I don't like things being comped that shouldn't be," I explained.

"After I leave, you can do whatever you want," he said. He was nearing his quit date.

I didn't respond, but I thought to myself, *"Whatever, Chad. Say what you want."* He hadn't even been in the restaurant during the lamb incident; he was rarely there. He hadn't been running the restaurant for months. I was. Yet here he came in out of nowhere trying to tell me how to handle a situation he knew nothing about. I was still trying to keep a professional work relationship. But the reality was I had been doing whatever I wanted for the past three years—well, for my entire life.

A couple days later, I was at the George, sitting next to a group of cooks from Sweet Basil as they discussed their general manager. Although I was yet to become a part of the conversation, just hearing the title of "general manager" got my blood boiling.

I was quick to butt in with, "Fuck our general manager. He'll never eat my food again!" With an attempt to control my temper, I settled down a bit, before I continued, "I feel bad for him because everyone in the world is going to want to eat our food, but that fucking piece of shit can generally eat a dick!"

In the restaurant, I tried to be professional, but I also made sure everyone knew I wasn't a pushover. I wanted to make sure everyone knew we were a chef-driven restaurant. Chad pissed me off, and I didn't give a fuck that he was our general manager. A few days later, Chad was managing when the restaurant suddenly got busy. He walked in the kitchen as I was on expo, and he told me I needed to focus on service.

I calmly responded, "It's your last day. Why don't you get the fuck out of the kitchen?" Those were the last words I ever said to him.

The truth was I was already feeling the pressures associated with being a general manager. I felt responsible for more than just the food. I cared about the overall success of the restaurant, in addition to truly wanting the best possible dining experience for our guests. There's an old adage that the customer is always right. I only believed this to be true if the customer was willing to pay.

I once had a Dover sole cooked four times until the guest was finally happy. I'll admit it probably shouldn't have taken four tries, but when we finally got it right, the guest could finally enjoy his meal. The guest was an older gentleman who undoubtedly knew food. He knew exactly how he liked his fish prepared. The guest was, in fact, right. We had not seared the fish properly. I accepted the blame for not giving my cook the correct guidance, but food costs were the least of my worries as long as the guest was happy.

By springtime, I was positive our entire staff was breaking up. My hopes, dreams, and expectations for our master sommelier all but completely vanished when he dislocated his elbow snowboarding and didn't have insurance. In addition to his injury, Roland was also expecting his first child. So if his physical issues weren't enough, he now also had financial stress, along with parenting responsibilities.

In addition, our entire front and back of house looked burnt out. Sexy Lexi said she was beginning to feel like she was over her head and talking about how she needed to go line cook somewhere. AJ was clearly just waiting it out for the season to end. I could tell he was feeling the pressures of running the kitchen. Tyson was under negotiations to be our new executive chef, although I knew he wasn't going to take it. He had explained to me that now was not the time for him to push it. He had already done that when he was younger, and he now had a family to take care of. I knew he was leaving us, too.

We had, for the most part, kept the same staff together for two years, which was pretty much unheard of at La Tour. But it was obvious that everyone was over it. Chef Paul, Lourdes, and I knew everyone was checked out. We were ready to flip the switch and start over from scratch. AJ went on vacation during the spring Taste of Vail Food and Wine Festival, which was an obvious I-don't-give-a-fuck move. While he was on vacation, Chef Paul told him to just "stay on vacation." When Chad also put in his full month notice, Lourdes didn't bother having him work it out either.

However, while everyone else was burning out, I was regaining my enthusiasm. La Tour was about to have a major staff overhaul. And I was more than ready for it to happen. It was time for us to change the culture in the restaurant.

It had been a *really* long three years, but the last six months felt extra long. Our team, although experienced, stuck together six months too long. I couldn't wait for them to leave. La Tour was finally my restaurant again, just like when it was Thomas and I.

I missed those days. But I had moved on, and now I was prepared to make a serious push. The excitement and energy I originally had when I began at La Tour had been renewed. I was back on my mission to change the way we dine in Vail.

# Chapter 16:

## Return to the Glory Years

Chef Paul was in the office one afternoon when I approached him and mentioned that I deserved a raise. Just for good measure, I added, "How 'bout a promotion, too?" I implied chef de cuisine or executive sous. I was eager to take on more responsibilities.

Chef Paul said he'd talk to Tyson. Tyson was still in negotiations about being promoted to our executive chef, even though I knew he wasn't taking it. So just as Thomas had done three years earlier, Tyson approached me and struck up a casual conversation. Then he asked me how much I wanted to be paid to be the chef de cuisine. A few days later, Chef Paul discreetly told me he had gotten me the raise I asked for. No promotion. Just the money.

We found the perfect executive chef: Sammy. Sammy was exactly what we were looking for. He had loads of experience and the type of experience that would benefit La Tour the most. Having worked corporate, Sammy was good with numbers. Balancing the numbers in La Tour was essential to our success. We were a small, independent operation. In addition to being good with numbers, Sammy had also worked in a Michelin-starred restaurant in France. So he also knew what it was like to work in high-pressure situations while maintaining high standards.

We promoted a guy named Pacquiao to be our newest sous

chef. Pacquiao (not his real name), unlike me, was a true Filipino born and raised on the island of Luzon. He was in his early twenties and inexperienced, but as long as we groomed him right, I believed he was prepared to make the jump to sous. Chef Paul also promoted Kai to be our new beverage director. Kai had been with La Tour for a while now, nearly as long as I had. I used to give him shit for always having blood-shot eyes, thinking he was really high at work. Hailing from Hawaii, Kai was a surfer, a really passionate one, too. Apparently it was just all that damn salt water in the eyes that made them a constant blood-shot red.

Chef Paul, Lourdes, and Sammy got together one afternoon and looked over our numbers. They concluded we only needed to do an extra seventeen covers for dinner to make up the revenue lost if we stopped doing lunch. Everyone hated doing lunch, so we made this our prime objective. We were once again dinner only, just like in La Tour's glory years.

It was time for La Tour to make a serious push, and I was ready to give it everything I had. Sammy had put me solely in charge of the specials and the tasting menus, as he had too many other things to worry about. Which was exactly how I wanted it. It felt like I had my own restaurant—although having my own restaurant was never my mission. On one of my days off, I sent out a group email to Chef Paul, Sammy, and the other managers about my new menu ideas. I was simply throwing out ideas, most of which weren't too carefully thought out, but one that struck Sammy's eye was a sweetbread dish. I thought it would suit the style of food we were serving.

Although the dish was well received by both Sammy and Chef Paul, Chef Paul made the executive decision to have the dish put on our specials page. I wasn't offended by the decision, but I began to realize Chef Paul wanted my creations to be kept separate from La Tour's. I tremendously admired Chef Paul, so I saw his decision in a positive light. Chef Paul was still grooming me to become my own independent chef.

As we were slowly grooming Pacquiao into becoming a chef, we put him in charge of the family meals, including the ordering. We had him make a weekly family meal calendar. With the calendar, Sammy also gave him a strict budget to follow. Not only that, none of us let Pacquiao just stick to what he knew. We asked for variety in our meals, requiring him to research dishes he'd never made before, making him leave his comfort zone. It was a well thought-out strategy. Having to budget and cater for his restaurant family, Pacquiao was on his way to becoming a successful chef.

Deciding not to serve lunch anymore didn't mean we didn't have to worry about money, though. We were pinching every penny even harder. We now had new tables, replacing that horrible brown paper. But we were still renting all our kitchen towels from a local company. We decided to save money and own our own towels outright. Owning our towels meant we had to wash them ourselves, too. Every day we had to soak the towels in bleach, ring them out (so they were lighter) at the end of the night, put them into trash bags, and store the bags in bins outside so animals like bears wouldn't tear them up and so the restaurant didn't stink. Someone would eventually take the towels to the laundromat to wash them.

One day we ran out of towels and had to handwash a few for service. Pacquiao threw them in the oven to dry. Then he forgot about them. By the time we found them, they were burnt to a crisp and stiff as cardboard.

I yelled at Pacquiao, "You know we have a timer for that shit?"

We also joked about having a marketing department. In reality, we were the marketing department. If any of us found any free time, we would bake cookies for the concierges. Then one of us would walk around delivering them to the nearby hotels. That was our way to promote the restaurant. Trying to save money was our main priority. Everyone, not just me, was now taking ownership of La Tour.

After two years of quite frankly too many chefs, it was now just Sammy, me, and Pacquiao leading the kitchen. That was all we needed, and all I really wanted. Our staff was young and inexperienced, and I liked that. Our staff was international, too. And I loved that!

After taking a break, an understandable one, my favorite trio of Mexicans were even back. It turned out they actually weren't even from Mexico, but from Peru. Being dark-skinned and speaking Spanish, our ignorant staff had made a stupid assumption. We did have Mexicans, though! Anna, one of my favorites, worked on pantry and couldn't speak a single word of English. She never let the communication barrier slow her down. In fact, it sped her up. She only communicated when something was important, and she spoke with gestures. If I heard her voice, I always looked her way. Working with her was efficient.

We had a quadruple serving of Serbians, too, including Miholo, the always-happy ladies man—I never saw him without at least three by his side. Girls loved the guy. How did he do it? Oh yeah, with that great attitude and by always being happy. People liked being around that, I guess. We also had the Eastern European power couple, Mia and Mike. His real name wasn't even

Mike; it was something foreign we couldn't pronounce, so we just called him Mike.

I finally had my international staff, reminiscent of the internationally diverse group Geranium was so proud of. Our staff was young, too. Real young! At forty years old, I was the oldest, an ancient dinosaur in a young man's industry. Sammy was a close second, but he needed to be. Sammy was our new leader; he needed that experience. No other person was even over thirty.

Except for our hardworking dishwasher who's real name was McLovio, but Pacquaio nicknamed McLovin from the *Superbad* movies. As a comic relief for the kitchen, he fit the nickname perfectly. McLovio was old (nearly twice everyone else's age). He knew he was old. We accepted the fact he was old. He showed up to work every day and never bitched. He spoke in the third person, too. I liked that about him. It made him sound like "the man." McLovio was the man. Even with his limited English, he got a kick out of being called McLovin. He knew what that meant.

And then that "book" everyone likes to go by? The book that says, "La Tour's too tough, too stressful, and that Chef Paul's a dick!" The new staff threw it out the window. *You think Chef Paul's a dick? What's that make you then? His bitch? That's right. You're a pussy! How's that make you feel?*

We made our own rules. We loved La Tour, and that Chef Paul was the man.

Three years earlier, I had returned from Europe on a mission to change the way we dined in Vail. I wanted to cook with passion. I wanted to be in a kitchen where everyone was happy. The past six months we hadn't been a happy kitchen. We were a kitchen divided. There was a lot of shit-talking behind each other's backs. It felt like everything Thomas had taught me about leadership was lost. But now, my dream was once again in my sights, and I couldn't have been more excited.

While my role at La Tour hadn't changed much since I had been there, I finally found a chef who could allow a lot of my visions to come true. Sammy and I both loved taking a lot of pressure off our cooks to put it on ourselves. We felt we were the strongest in the kitchen, so we embraced the challenge. We began plating a lot of the dishes on expo. Sammy loved meticulous plating, and I considered plating to be his strength. We asked the cooks to focus on cooking properly, particularly the proteins. Make sure they hit the temps on their steaks. Sear that foie properly, then put it in the window. We'd finish it from there.

I also brought in my two personal induction burners and immersion blender. On expo, we could now cook, finish sauces, emulsify, or froth sauces. Expo became the most active station in the kitchen—and it often was a two-man operation. We also bought a small deep-fryer at Walmart that was often set up on expo. Sammy shared my same ambitions. We had the same work ethic. Sammy knew food well and was opinionated, too, both important qualities of a successful chef.

Upon Sammy's arrival, his main focus was on kitchen improvements. At this point, we had done none. Except I'd had my buddy, Carl, weld some of our drawers that fell apart. I repaid him with a free meal.

Sammy was in the office one day and someone from Sweet Basil stopped in to drop off an invitation to an open house. Sweet Basil had just remodeled its kitchen for its fortieth anniversary. It was about Sweet Basil's tenth kitchen remodel, too. I honestly didn't want to go. I knew Sweet Basil had a nice kitchen. Everyone knew. I didn't want to see what we couldn't have. I think

Sammy was the opposite; he believed we could get some up-grades. He wanted to see if there were any ideas we could use to improve our kitchen.

Although I wasn't really into it, I went for the free food. I had recently poached their Christmas party, so I didn't have a problem enjoying their food—especially for free. The last time I had actually been in that kitchen was fifteen years earlier when Argentinian Danny worked there. The kitchen had changed tremendously since then. But what I saw that made me the most jealous was that they not only had a tilt braiser, but also a stove specifically for making stocks. The stove was only a foot off the ground. Just hours earlier, I had picked up a twenty-gallon pot and hoisted it three feet off the ground to put it on our grill (the only place it would fit). Those bastards got it easy!

We loved to joke about it, but Sammy did get a little something to improve our kitchen. We had a stainless steel table in our pantry section where the majority of our plating would be done, particularly for large parties. The table was being held up by small metal pans, as the legs were broken. One night, Sammy bumped into the table and it collapsed onto him.

Two months after Sammy threw a small kitchen fit, we finally got a new table. It cost about two hundred bucks. It was no stock stove or tilt braiser, but we were pretty stoked.

As for the front of house, Kai had the most enthusiasm of anyone I had yet to see in that position. Kai was four certifications away from being a master sommelier. In other words, he never took a single wine test. I could tell his real passion was cocktails. With cocktails, Kai could express his creativity. Our cocktail list was frequently changing. I could tell Kai loved having the freedom to experiment. He was our first beverage director to begin incorporating CBD (a non-psychoactive component of cannabis and hemp) into our drinks. He also experimented with a lot of different textures and presentations. Kai was thinking of drinks with the same thought process I used to create my dishes.

Kai had the same philosophy as I did: He didn't need a piece of paper for validation that he was good. He was self-confident enough to make mistakes, learn from them, and trust his palate to improve his own ideas. Our old master sommelier, Roland, had been teaching Kai too, so he had the help he needed. He was committed, wanted to learn, and showed tremendous passion.

Kai also began hosting wine classes for our staff. The wine classes would really bring the team together. I did my best to make it to every class, inviting our line cooks to join us. Not serving lunch made that possible. I was learning about wine; our entire staff was. We didn't just limit the classes to our own staff either. Everyone in the industry was invited. The classes brought Vail Valley's entire restaurant industry together. And we were having fun, too.

The first wine dinner we did together as a team was probably my favorite night of service in my entire career. There is no better feeling than an extremely busy night that runs smoothly. I was working expo, and Sammy was acting as a float between stations. The pantry station was usually the station that needed the most help, but not because of the lack of experience or having our weakest cook.

In many French restaurants, pantry is the station that needs to be mastered first before moving on to sous chef. In the states, however, it's the opposite. Here, most cooks actually start out on pantry before moving up the line. I feel this is simply a testosterone- and ego-driven move, especially in a male-heavy industry. Experienced cooks want to cook with fire, serve the more expensive dishes, and be where all the action is.

But pantry is where the real excitement is. The dishes are intricate and the most complex, causing the station to usually be the busiest. Despite the lower price of the dishes, I feel the station is the most important. Pantry serves the first and last impressions of the meal. While entrees generally cost more, their compositions are usually less complex and intricate. Furthermore, working the hot line, you are cooking food. The general rule when cooking is to not play with it, just let it sit and cook. This allows for you to buy time. You can set up plates and do other tasks. On pantry, there's no buying time. A ticket comes in and your hands are constantly moving, constantly building one dish after another. Always active, it's a very tough station.

For the wine dinner, Sammy had decided to serve beignets for dessert. This required for a deep fryer to be set up on expo, adding an extra responsibility for me running the pass. During service, I was staring at six feet worth of tickets, nearly all of which were having the five-course wine dinner menu. I was so busy I didn't even have time to move tickets around. I would just scan the tickets and mark them off as the courses would go out. This kept the tickets in order, which allowed me to prioritize. As the tickets would be completed, I would call, "Service." Previously, we had been calling out "pick up" when food needed to get run. The next day, during our pre-shift meeting, I explained to the staff why I had changed the call. I explained to them that "service" is a classier, more elegant way of saying it. Otherwise, we might as well be a diner. I could just be back there ringing a fucking bell, yelling "Order up, hot food, come and get it!"

I knew our guests could hear everything. Displaying proper dinner etiquette and manners, I wanted them to believe their food was being prepared by cooks with class. Just as we had been judged a few years earlier by our host flashing her boobs, I knew our guests had the right to judge us by anything they wanted to. I wanted our young staff to understand that every little detail mattered. We needed to display the same type of class we expected from our guests.

This summer at La Tour, we had a restaurant review that was meaningful for me. I was chasing after global recognition for La Tour. Although not global recognition, I felt this was a start, a sign we were moving in the right direction. In a "Best Things Colorado" article, Madison Dragna reviewed the top ten French restaurants in Colorado. Making it on a list as one of the best restaurants in Colorado wasn't the only reason the review meant a lot to me. In the review, Madison wrote, "Unique menu options are always being added to this ever-changing menu. Enjoy well-made seafood and duck along with classic French dishes infused with Asian flair."

It wasn't much, but without having to mention my name, this was the first time I knew a review was talking about me. I took a lot of pride in constantly changing my dishes, a reason why I may never have a "signature dish." The review also was the first time I realized that I actually had a specific style of food. "Classic French with an Asian flair." My dishes had personality now. It was no longer "That's a La Tour dish." It was now "That's a Paul-Asian dish."

La Tour was finally becoming the restaurant I envisioned it could become. We may have been working our butts off, but we were having fun doing it. I was especially enjoying conquering all our challenges. It gave me a true sense of accomplishment. Out of everything we were doing, I was probably the proudest of our family meals. Pacquiao deserved much of the credit, but we were all working extra hard to be able to sit down together as a family and enjoy a meal together.

Our family meals were even becoming international, too. Pacquiao was great at cooking Filipino comfort foods, such as adobo and picadillo. This reminded me of home, my mom's cooking. I had long missed my mom's cooking, and Pacquiao could replicate it to near perfection. We also had Serbian Sundays, with the front of house help of Mia, Mike, and Miholo serving up specialties from their homeland. I once again was able to enjoy dishes I'd first come across on my trip to Croatia. Dishes such as ćevapčići with ajvar, the little fingers with a red pepper-eggplant relish. This was heaven. Although we couldn't always travel the world, we had brought the world to our kitchen. Our team was becoming a close family, too. There was no longer that great divide between front of house, back of house, and management, all by simply sharing a meal together.

With new leadership in the kitchen, Chef Paul decided to order new chef coats. However, this time, the new chef coats had our names on them without our titles. For me, this was a subtle move for equality in the kitchen. Even our newly hired line cooks would get their names sewn into their jackets, which I considered our biggest move. Having my name on my jacket meant very little to me; I already knew my importance to the team. But imagine being a nineteen-year-old kid and having your name on a jacket next to the La Tour logo. Any degenerate off the street would instantly have renewed confidence and increased self-esteem. Young cooks had an instant increase in pride; they felt important and part of the team. Putting everyone's name on their jacket, just like the chefs', was a small gesture that suggested everyone check their egos at the door. Although we understood hierarchy was important for our ideas to come to fruition, everyone had a feeling that their ideas could be heard. Equality like this was a concept I had witnessed in Copenhagen and dreamed of making a reality within the states.

I had been suffering from a chronic cough for more than a year now. I heard if you have a cough for more than two weeks, you should go see a doctor. But I have always hated doctors. I felt I knew my body better than they did. But I really wanted to figure out why I had this cough, so I went to Doctors On Call in nearby Avon.

Doctors always check your vitals as standard practice, and they diagnosed me with high blood pressure. The doctor then prescribed me some drugs for my cough, while asking me questions concerning my blood pressure, such as, "What do you do for work? Do you drink?" I explained to him that I was a chef and told him that yes, I drank quite often.

He continued, "Yeah, it's very common for chefs to drink a lot." He asked me to cut back on my drinking for a week and come back for a free follow-up to see if my cough went away.

The following week, I had just closed the restaurant and was walking toward The George for my customary after-work drinks. I didn't necessarily feel like having a drink, so I checked my phone to see what time it was. I realized the bus was about to leave, so it was perfect timing for me to just go home. As I ran up the long double set of stairs and through the Transportation Center, just as I was exiting through the doors on the other side, I fainted. I quickly came to and was on my knees struggling to breathe, as though I had just knocked the wind out of myself. I had a nasty black eye and a large bump on my head.

When I returned to the doctor to follow up on my cough, he quickly noticed my black eye. Obviously, the first thing he wanted to know was what had happened. I explained, and he asked if I had cut back on my drinking. I shrugged my shoulders, thinking I did, after all, take at least that one night off. The whole time, the doctor was staring at his computer. I was sitting in the chair and could feel my heart racing even faster. With the doctor looking perplexed, I could feel my blood boiling. I wanted to kick his ass. He had no idea that he was causing me to have even higher blood pressure. I had come here to find out why I had a cough, and all he did was prescribe me drugs. Sure, the drugs could get rid of my cough, but why was I coughing in the first place? Not only did the doctor not tell me why I had a cough, but also couldn't tell me why I had fainted. I considered him to be a useless, expensive idiot. I just wanted answers.

As soon as I left the office, I called my parents, knowing they were in the medical field. I explained to them what the doctor had told me. Not even needing to examine me, they told me the cough was because I had allergies. That was all I needed to know. They told me all I needed to do was get some Allegra DM, an over-the-counter solution. My parents gave me the answers I was looking for.

I proceeded to tell them about my high blood pressure and how I had fainted, giving myself a black eye. My mom actually kind of chuckled, a sign I was perfectly fine. I, indeed, had high blood pressure, just not of a major concern. Stressing while trying to catch my bus made my heart work harder than it should have, causing me to faint. I was new to the smartphone world (I'd only had one for a few months), so she went on to say there was even an app I could get for my phone to help monitor my blood pressure. This experience made me hate doctors even more. I wanted to understand the root of the problem, not just be handed drugs. That wasn't a real solution.

# Chapter 17:

## Chasing the Dream

I was walking with The Hippie one evening when she mentioned she had some friends in town having dinner at La Botega and we should go meet up with them. When we arrived at the restaurant, The Hippie introduced me to her Swedish friend Ijah. Ijah explained to me that she was a professional dancer and was often in Vegas for work. She danced at special events all over the world. I told her I loved Vegas and we should exchange numbers. I offered to meet her out there the next time she was working.

She went on to tell me how she lived in Miami and had gotten a spare bedroom just so she could have friends visit. I knew I had paid vacation coming up so I began looking for cheap flights—to pretty much anywhere. I wasn't sure where I wanted to go, but then I found a cheap ticket to Miami. It was only the week after I had met Ijah, so I think I caught her a little off guard how quickly I was visiting. Regardless, I took her up on her offer of a free place to stay.

I arrived at Ijah's apartment, a tall highrise in Miami Beach, and checked in with security so I could get buzzed up. I wasn't used to this kind of security. I thought to myself, "This must have been how Vivian felt in *Pretty Woman*."

After several flight delays, it was already four in the morning.

Ijah and her roommate were both still up, a good sign. I could tell they were night owls, which suited me perfectly. I never found out what her roommate did, but knowing Ijah was a dancer, it didn't come as a surprise she stayed up late. I was hungry from the long day traveling so we went to get some burgers. I was stoked I could still get real food at this hour.

On the way, we walked along the beach. There is nothing more peaceful than the beach at night. Here I was, enjoying what we often make fun of: long walks on the beach with a beautiful girl. Although guys often joke about it and I had just met Ijah, it really was kind of romantic walking on that beach. As we were enjoying our burgers, Ijah asked me what I wanted to do during my visit. I told her I wanted to relax on the beach and eat good food. So that was exactly what we did. I told her I planned on taking her out to a nice dinner for giving me a free place to stay. I felt I could afford it since I had saved hundreds by not having to pay for a hotel room.

As I searched for restaurants, I decided I wanted something nice but also fun. Nothing too pretentious. I decided on Bazaar Mar by Jose Andres. (This location has since closed.) Jose Andres had become world-renowned for his innovation, even earning Michelin stars in the process. Bazaar Mar turned out to be the perfect choice, bright and playful, with large ceramic sculptures of fish protruding out of the walls. It was nothing like the seriousness of La Tour, and that's what I wanted. I was in Miami to have a good time, and this restaurant was just that.

I was disappointed that I couldn't try many of the unique dishes that I wanted to. The fish were just too rare and not always available. Fish such as lionfish, which they caught using a spear. The "California funnel cake" did impress though. Based on a common California roll, this was an original and unique rendition. The ingredients were the same, but the base was a seaweed-rice cracker made in the style of a funnel cake, served high off the table on a stand so you could easily pick it up and take a bite. The dish was funky and fun. No table manners or proper etiquette was needed. This was the ideal dinner for me and Ijah to enjoy, as we shared everything.

After dinner, we spent the rest of the night out on the town, literally until the sun came up. We passed through the art district, a park with commissioned graffiti. I've always appreciated that kind of abstract, freehanded, often spontaneous art. We walked by a bar just as a drag show was starting and thought, "Why not?" Drag queens can put on quite a show! We enjoyed daiquiris at a nearby tiki bar, which really made me feel like I was somewhere tropical. We sang a hot duet at karaoke: "The Time of My Life" from *Dirty Dancing*. And we danced! Ijah was shocked to see that I actually could dance. It's amazing how your body can move when you are happy.

I had fallen in love with Miami.

Growing up, I had never really liked Florida. My parents would take me there, visiting Epcot Center and Walt Disney World. I always thought of Florida as too hot, too humid. I loved Florida now, especially Miami. Ijah's apartment had amazing views and a prime location, and she and her roommate were welcoming and made me feel at home. After Vail and Vegas, I now considered Miami to be my third home.

My next paid time off, I decided to visit Ijah in Miami again. Ijah had explained to me how she had a thousand dollars in singles in her room, I assumed from being a dancer. She suggested that we should go to a strip club. I thought that was a great idea, so I bought a hundred ones off of her. On our way to the massive, 75,000-square-foot, two-level club, Tootsie's, Ijah decided to call her friend Tasia to join us. Tasia, a hot blonde, was a dancer and model from Russia and was now living in Atlanta. They had recently met while dancing for an event together.

As we arrived at the club, I asked Tasia if she wanted to join me at the stage and "make it rain" on some dancers. As we sat down by the stage, the cocktail waitress asked us what we would like to drink.

Tasia responded, "I'll have a Hennessy."

I thought to myself, "This is my kinda girl," and I ordered myself the same. After we finished "making it rain," we got in Tasia's brand new Mercedes and headed to a late-night club. While we were cruising down the highway, Tasia mentioned how she had never hit a hundred in her car. As I rode shotgun, tightly gripping the oh-shit handle, I thought, "It's four in the morning. We've been drinking Hennessy all night. Now is not the time to see if your car does a hundred." That didn't stop her from trying.

After (miraculously safely) reaching the club, we got out of the car. Ijah and I decided to call it a night and go home. As we jumped in an Uber, Ijah apologized to me, saying, "Sorry, if I knew she was that immature, I would have never had us get in that car." This was when I realized I actually had been living the rock star lifestyle of my eighties heroes. I had, in fact, finally found my own Tawny Kitaen.

La Tour's twentieth anniversary was quickly approaching. We decided to run throwback dishes, things Chef Paul served during his early years. Angelee was on our patio enjoying bottomless mimosas. I joined, sharing sips, as she constantly reminded me, "They're bottomless."

She had just sent a text to Chef Paul congratulating him on his twentieth anniversary. She then told me that she not only worked at La Tour during the late nineties and early 2000s, but she also returned to work there for a second time. This gave me a sense of how long ago that really was. A sense of how far La Tour had come, how far I had come. Angelee reminded me of how we'd had dinner at Terra Bistro and how much fun we'd had. I agreed. We'd had a great time.

I went on to tell her how I had eaten at Pierre Gagnaire's and suggested the two of us should fly to Vegas and have dinner at Guy Savoy's, another highly acclaimed French chef. As I pronounced his name in English, Angelee knew French and pronounced it correctly. She then explained that the throwback dish we were serving, *Salmon Feuille de Brick*, was the dish that had put Lyon, France, on the culinary map. The legendary Chef Paul Bocuse's hometown. I had been at La Tour trying to make my own huge push for global recognition. I wanted my own *Salmon Feuille de Brick*.

I was working the pass with Sammy one night, and we had a seventeen-top come in for dinner, ordering a prix-fixe menu. When the order came in, Anna said something in Spanish. I looked over and she was holding up the container where she held her *tuiles* (baked wafers). She didn't have enough. I relayed the message to Sammy, who instructed me to gather the *mise*. I grabbed a hotel pan and ran through the parking garage to our dry storage and gathered the ingredients.

As I returned, Sammy asked, "How long until you get the batter together?"

I quickly scanned over the recipe and replied, "Three minutes."

Sammy called back, "Bake off like six. The entrees just ran. You have about ten minutes."

I began searching for a Tamis to sift the flour through. "Where's the fucking Tamis?" I asked. I looked at Anna and tried to reiterate it in my best Spanglish: "Donde pinche fucking..." I paused, not knowing how to translate "Tamis."

More time passed, and we still couldn't find it. Anna said something in Spanish and pointed to a chinois.

"Fuck it," I calmly replied and dumped the pre-measured flour onto a sheet of parchment. With the mixer running, I held the top down with my elbow, as the latch was broken. I folded the parchment in half and carefully but quickly poured in the flour. As I was finishing the batter, Anna again said something in Spanish. I looked over. She had set up a sheet tray with a silpat on it for me to spread the batter out on. She then put her hands up, as to ask what else she could do to help. I moved my hand in a motion, as if I were spreading something out. I was hoping for a spatula, but Anna sprayed nonstick spray on the silpat.

I finished the batter and ran to the oven. Yanking the temperature knob down, I called out, "Turning the oven down."

I went to spread the batter and it slid all over the greased silpat. Sammy ran to the oven, correctly adjusting the temperature and called back, "The oven's at 350."

I flipped the silpat over and spread out the batter. Then called out, "Where'd I put my fucking nuts? I just had them."

Our newly hired sous chef, Nathan, found my nuts and handed them to me, saying, "Deez nuts?"

I sprinkled the nuts over my batter and put them in the oven. Sammy called back, "Setting a timer for three minutes." I set up the pantry station to form the *tuiles*, angling a trash can to support a large sheet tray, and placed a fresh tray on top. The timer went off, I pulled the tuiles out of the oven and placed the hot pan on top of the fresh tray. As I was forming the fresh, warm tuiles over metal bars, the first round of desserts was leaving the kitchen.

I closed down the kitchen that night and began my weekend, once again suffering from insomnia. When I returned from my weekend, I was standing in the kitchen and felt that horribly familiar, weird vertigo feeling. This time I didn't need my staff to tell me I shouldn't be there.

A few days passed, and I was still suffering from insomnia. I hadn't slept in five or six days, when I got a call from Ijah. She was in town with another one of her dancer friends and wanted to meet up. I probably should have said no, but I met up anyway, and we decided to have dinner at La Tour. But I couldn't eat. Insomnia left me without an appetite.

As it turned out, dinner with two beautiful girls would be my final "farewell" meal at La Tour.

The following day, I met with Chef Paul, Lourdes, and Sammy and turned in my key. It was an extreme roller coaster of a meeting, from me nearly crying like a child and begging to keep my job, to then ecstatically throwing my keys at them. I had no control over my mind and body.

As I adjusted to life without a job, I sent a group text to Chef Paul and the other managers at La Tour.

"Don't worry about me," I wrote. "La Tour has a staff now."

Chef Paul replied, "Thank you."

Nothing else needed to be said. After dedicating the past four years of my life to the restaurant, I knew La Tour didn't need me anymore.

I was skating through the village one afternoon, something I hadn't done in the last four years, when my sister-in-law called me up. She was concerned. I had displayed odd behavior, she said: weird posts on social media, and I had even called my brother in the middle of the night. I was showing obvious signs I was looking for help. Amy asked me what I was up to.

"Currently, I'm skateboarding through town," I said. I was specific.

After I hung up the phone, the vertigo returned, hitting me hard, and I knew I was in serious trouble. Although her intentions were good, Amy had scared me, making me question if I actually was all right. I sent Amy a text rather than a phone call, because I knew the vertigo would make it difficult to have a conversation. It would make my brain work too hard.

My text was straight to the point: "I just had a weird vertigo feeling. I'm at the Evergreen Lodge, room 103."

That was all I said. I felt like I could easily go over the edge and not be able to recover. I was fighting extremely hard to keep my sanity. It was the scariest feeling of my life.

My brother called me back and said he would be on the first flight in the morning to get me. I had checked myself into the Evergreen Lodge the night before, so I went back to my room and stayed there until I was saved. My credit card had been declined at two other fancy hotels. Fighting with my brain, I thought I was rich.

When my brother arrived to pick me up, he said he was sure I had a chemical imbalance in my blood. He was certain I was manic-depressive. Both he and my sister had struggled with the same thing. He knew the drugs I needed to feel better. After I took the pills he handed me, we drove back to Minnesota. He decided to drive us back rather than fly, because he figured the long drive would be better for both of us. It would help clear our minds. Being forced into a conversation is stressful. The peaceful, long drive would relieve some stress, and we both knew it.

When we arrived in Minnesota, I was just in time for my dad's eightieth birthday. It was great to see my parents again. This was the greatest part of my journey. I had hardly seen my parents over the past twenty years. My parents often objected to many of my life choices, but they had always supported me. The fact that they even still talked to me after how rebellious I was spoke loudly enough. They showed me unconditional love, especially when I needed it the most. We'd never had a conversation that didn't end with, "I love you." It was a tough journey (probably for them, too), and I couldn't have done it without them.

We celebrated my dad's birthday at my brother's cabin up north, hanging out on the lake with my family. My oldest nephew was now a college graduate with a beautiful girlfriend. My strongest memories of him were when he was four, still holding my hand to cross the street. I now had a young niece, too. I had been described as the "mysterious uncle." Having never even met, I was a myth to her.

Minnesota never felt like home, but it felt like it now. I got to Jet Ski again, on a Kawasaki 800SX-R, an upgrade from my childhood. I'd never lost my passion for it. I had simply forgotten about my passion.

After the party, my parents drove me back down to Jackson and took me to see a doctor. Before the doctor came out to question me, my dad instructed me to make it sound worse than I really was, to make sure I got the prescription I needed. He had long been retired and no longer was licensed to write prescriptions himself. My condition had been bad, but by this time, I had already settled down. Although I was capable of handling the early stages, I needed the drugs as a security blanket. It was obvious to my entire family I was bipolar. Before my brother saved me, I was close to being put in a mental hospital. After questioning me, the doctor concluded I didn't have a mental illness and handed me a one-time prescription to Lorazepam, to help with anxiety.

While in Jackson, I got a hotel room, as my parents had sold the house I had grown up in. They now lived on the lake that I grew up Jet-Skiing on as a kid, and my childhood house was too far away. My parents tore down the old cabin and built a new home. All my old ramps were gone. There were very few memories of my childhood, except one. My parents had held onto one of my beloved Kawasaki 550sxes. When I was a kid, my parents had given me one as a present, and they couldn't let it go.

I stayed in a hotel room, because I wanted to walk through my old neighborhood. I wanted to see downtown Jackson again. While I was walking through my old neighborhood, I realized how much Jackson had grown. My house was no longer a block from a cornfield, but now several blocks. My neighborhood was now four times larger than when I had grown up there. And those hills I used to bomb with Sean as a kid didn't look nearly as big as I remembered them. Call it cliche, but it was true. Even the most intimidating hill was tiny.

Jackson had its own little skatepark, too. The kids who lived there now didn't have to steal wood to build their own ramps, and I certainly didn't see any pre-teens skating on rooftops. Those were some of my greatest memories. It was now time to inspire a new generation. Just like my eighties idols had inspired me.

I eventually returned to Vail. There, I had the humbling re-alization I was, in fact, all grown up. My joints are missing so much cartilage I can now feel winter coming months before the first snowfall. My whole body aches, and I realize I probably fell on my head a few too many times. Although I'm still not a fan of doctors, I really did need that Lorazepam. Other than that, I now kind of hate drugs. Except for cocaine. Cocaine is a party drug. I just hope they never legalize it. I like how it's expensive and hard to get.

My financial situation caught up to me, as well. I never really could afford the rock star lifestyle I was living. Now, I'm okay with that. I don't really want to *achieve* all my dreams. I want to know what it feels like to *chase* after them.

I am still chasing global recognition. I don't want to have three Michelin stars. I want to know what it *feels* like to chase af-ter them. Chasing after your dreams is where all the excitement is. It's not sitting at the top with nowhere to go. I still have dreams of someday being Al Pacino in *Scarface*, too.

My life has been a crazy ride, and I've enjoyed every minute of it. Just like Whitesnake used to sing to me, I guess "here I go again." I'm starting over, and this new story's just beginning.

I hope you enjoyed my story. If so please leave a review by either using this link or scanning the QR code

https://www.amazon.com/review/create-review/?ie=UT-F8&channel=glance-detail&asin=B0CTHRBBHW

* 9 7 9 8 8 6 9 1 9 9 5 0 8 *